> *I beat this New Economy, and I can help you do the same. The techniques and tactics I share in this book will help end your unemployment.*
>
> – Dan Quillen, author of *Get a Job!*

PRAISE FOR *Get a Job!*

"I read every word of every page and could not put this book down! Combining a personal style with years of HR experience, Dan Quillen skillfully coaches the reader on every aspect of their job search, while addressing the very human component of the process. It is a highly-informative, honest and positive must-read for anyone seeking employment in today's troubled economy ... Even though I have 20-plus years of recruiting experience, I learned a few things too! I plan to buy a copy and will recommend it to candidates and colleagues."

Sharon Davis
Senior Recruiter
LAC Group

"Quillen covers some of the most critical elements of the job hunt in this New Economy. His advice and counsel hit the nail on the head, and if you are looking for work you would be well-advised to follow Dan's recommendations. Doing so will significantly increase your chance at landing a job in this difficult economy."

Sherri Hickman
Senior Placement Director
Special Counsel

"I firmly believe that with very few exceptions a résumé gets an interview and an interview gets the job. Over the years I cannot begin to count the number of résumés I have seen that would not get anyone anywhere but the archives (better known as the trash). Dan's book has so many truths regarding what actually happens when you submit your résumé for a job opportunity via HR software, gatekeepers, and executive assistants with excellent advice on success whatever the obstacles you will face with each job opportunity. If you want to spend your money wisely on creating a résumé that will result in interviews and therefore job offers, This book will take you further and more expeditiously than most so-called experts. He gives clear, simple, succinct direction in *Get a Job!* to create a résumé that will get the interview to get the job! Don't skip any chapters, they are all relevant and matter for your successful job search."

Ginny Ford
Ford Personnel, Inc.

D0290025

ABOUT THE AUTHOR

Dan Quillen has been a professional in Human Resources for more than twenty years. For a decade, he was the Director of Human Resources for one of the largest law firms in the western United States. Currently he is the Director of Internal Services (managing Human Resources, Purchasing, Risk and Fleet) for the City of Aurora, the third largest city in Colorado.

For years, Dan has been an active mentor for those who are out of work, freely sharing his expertise in résumé review and creation, interviewing and job searching. A few years ago Dan was laid off and had the opportunity to try the techniques he has been teaching others for years. In *Get a Job!,* Dan shares the knowledge and techniques that allowed him to find a job in a short period of time during the worst economic downturn our country has had since the Great Depression.

When not doing HR, Dan is a professional writer specializing in travel, technical, genealogy, and how-to subjects. He has written and published fourteen books on various topics. Dan makes his home in Centennial, Colorado. If you'd like to contact Dan about anything in this book, his e-mail address is: *wdanielquillen@gmail.com,* and he welcomes your comments and questions.

TABLE OF CONTENTS

1. WELCOME TO THE NEW ECONOMY

The key to growth is the introduction of higher dimensions of consciousness into our awareness. — Lao Tzu

Greetings, and thank you for purchasing this book. I know you have at least a few questions about me and how I can help, so let me answer them for you:

WHY IS THIS GUY QUALIFIED TO WRITE THIS BOOK?
I have been a Human Resources (HR) professional for more than twenty years, and all those years have been on the hiring manager side of the table – I know what hiring managers are looking for. I know what works, but perhaps more important, I know what doesn't work!

Like you, I lost my job in the midst of the worst economic environment this country has known since the Great Depression. Drawing on my knowledge and expertise, I was able to find a new job in a fraction of the time most job hunters are now experiencing.

And I am making that knowledge and expertise available to you through the pages of this book.

HOW IS THIS BOOK DIFFERENT FROM OTHERS ?
Good question – I am glad you asked! Here are a few things you'll find different from other books in this genre:

- I am a hiring manager, not a recruiter. I know what hiring managers think, what they are looking for.
- I have walked in your shoes during this terrible New Economy. I have walked in your shoes, and for the most part, *at the same time* you were walking in them yourself!

9

- I give you common-sense advice on how to prepare yourself emotionally and financially for your unemployment ordeal. Few books, if any, out there do that.
- I provide you information about what to expect from unemployment benefits at greater depth than any other book I am aware of.
- I provide a spreadsheet format that will help you organize your job search in the most effective manner.
- I use my personal experiences throughout the book, to help illustrate elements of job hunting. These are personal experiences I have had, some on the job seeker's side of the interview table, some on the hiring manager's side of the table.
- I am writing this *during* the New Economy! So much of the advice in other books out there is pre-New Economy, and it simply no longer works. New tactics and strategies are required in this New Economy in which we find ourselves.

WHY DID HE WRITE THIS BOOK?

The short answer is: I like to help people. The longer answer is: this *New Economy* is the worst job hunting climate our country has experienced since the Great Depression. In my more than two decades as an HR professional I have helped friends find work by reviewing their résumés and cover letters, doing mock interviews, providing job leads and offering my opinions about how to search for jobs.

And then – I was laid off.

Now I had the opportunity to try some of my own advice. The last time I had to actively look for a job as an external candidate was in 1979. I spent over two decades in the AT&T family of companies (AT&T, Lucent and Avaya), and didn't have a lot of experience on the outside looking (and trying to get) in.

Even though I had been doing HR for all those years, the latest economic downturn and new technology had changed the playing field for job searchers. Jobs that formerly attracted a dozen applicants were now attracting literally hundreds of applicants. My wife is a school teacher in the Denver, Colorado metropolitan area. Recently, her school had an opening for a first grade teacher. The principal posted the position at 8:30am. By noon there were over 300 applicants, and by the end of the day, over 400 individuals had applied. Eventually, nearly 1,000 hopeful applicants applied for the position. Unfortunately, that is not uncommon in the New Economy.

WHAT WILL I FIND IN THESE PAGES?

As I began my own job hunt in earnest, I discovered something that surprised me – the process had changed. I assumed a squeaky-clean résumé and a good cover letter would make me stand out from the rest of the job-seeking crowd. Boy – was I wrong! Job hunters had become more sophisticated, and hiring managers and HR departments had likewise become even more sophisticated. I learned quickly that a one-size-fits-all résumé simply wasn't cutting it — I needed a different résumé for every position I was targeting.

I also learned I couldn't do it alone. I needed the help of legions of friends and acquaintances, business associates and others. I needed to find the best websites for the positions I was seeking. I needed to spend full time on my job hunt. I needed to use social media to beat the competition.

> A squeaky-clean, one-size-fits-all résumé isn't all I need!

And make no mistake – the competition is substantial. The displaced workers in the New Economy are some of the best educated and best experienced ever to hit the streets looking for a job. Pressures from well-educated younger workers are also present, and in many cases they are vying for the same jobs you are. While you have 10, 15, 20 years more experience, you also command a higher salary. The temptation for employers in today's tight economy is to sacrifice experience for lower wages. That's a reality.

Whether you are currently unemployed, expecting to become unemployed, or simply interested in how best to find that next position, this book will provide valuable tips and tactics for you to be successful in your job search. Finally, I learned a tough lesson – age discrimination is alive and well in the market today. Later in this book, I'll provide you with some tactics to help get you in the door, and then overcome negative perceptions of older workers.

Through the pages of this book, I'll share with you the successes – and failures – I had during my job hunt.

So come along with me as we explore the nooks and crannies of the job-search market. Hopefully along the way you'll glean more than a few nuggets that will help you land a job, perhaps even your dream job.

2. OVERVIEW

The price of success is hard work, dedication to the job at hand, and the determination that whether we win or lose, we have applied the best of ourselves to the task at hand. — Vince Lombardi

We are about to begin a journey, you and I. Hopefully by following the various suggestions in this book, you will secure employment or will shortly do so. Here is what I will show you in this book:

This is a tough economy – the toughest since the Great Depression. Figures at the time of this writing indicate 23 million Americans are out of work or underemployed. Because of governmental spin, only about half of those are counted in the unemployment figures – 7 to 8 percent, but those of us with friends and family who are out of work know the real number is much higher.

In **Chapter 1**, *Welcome to the New Economy!*, I talk about the toxic employment environment we find ourselves in today. I share my credentials as both an HR professional with many years of experience – as well as a job-seeker myself in this New Economy. I encourage you to try some things I suggest even though they may take you out of your comfort zone.

In **Chapter 3**, *Plan to Stay, Prepare to Leave*, I share sage counsel I once heard from a leader in my company. It was sound counsel then, and even more so now. If you are in the throes of unemployment, it's too late to act on that. But you'll be employed again, and the lessons I learned and share as a result of that counsel may make a difference for you down the line. And if you are still employed, it may help you survive and even thrive if you are thrown into the unemployment pond and forced to learn to swim.

I discuss how to make yourself a crucial and contributing member of any employment community to which you belong, how to work in the "white spaces" – those areas that don't fit neatly into anyone's job descriptions. I talk about expanding your knowledge and skills within your company, and of expanding your intra-company networks.

Closing out the *Plan to Stay* section of the chapter, I cover whose responsibility promotions and progress within the company is – yours. Your boss may be a valuable resource for furthering your career, but at the end of the day, *you* are the one who must take charge of *your* career.

In the *Prepare to Leave* section, I address the importance of education, and the role it will likely play if you need to look for a job. I share strategies about how to further your education.

In Chapter 4, *What Do You Do Now*, I discuss first steps you would be wise to take should you become part of an unappetizing statistic – one of the nation's unemployed. I talk about how important having a positive attitude is in your job search. I share my methodology for organizing and keeping track of my job hunt.

I talk quite a bit about networking – its value and how to organize it, and share some of the things I did to reach out within my network. I spend a significant percentage of the chapter talking about various websites available to job seekers, and offer data specific to my own job search – job leads and interviews I received from which websites.

Working with recruiters is also addressed in this chapter. I talk about how to use them, and how to make it easy for them to represent you in your job search. The role and importance of job coaches is covered as well.

Perhaps most important, I recommend that you set a job search schedule for yourself to follow religiously. I share examples of how I set up my own job search – activities performed, times of the day and days of the week they were done, etc. I also counsel you to *Stay Busy!* in both your job hunt activities and other activities too. I also suggest you may want to put a moratorium on watching daytime TV or reading books during the times you could or should be looking for work.

The last section of this chapter discusses unemployment benefits, how and when to apply, and some thoughts about them.

In **Chapter 5**, *Social Networking*, I go over the value of using social media like LinkedIn, Facebook, and Twitter to expand your network and help you find jobs.

In **Chapter 6**, *Résumés*, I spend a great deal of time addressing this critical element in your job hunt arsenal. I share my thoughts as a hiring manager, someone who has looked at tens of thousands of résumés throughout my career. I have some strong opinions about résumés, and I offer those throughout the chapter. Perhaps the most important lesson here is that one-size-*doesn't*-fit-all any more when it comes to résumés. In today's job search market, each résumé must be tailored specifically to the requirements of the job for which you are applying. I share excerpts from my résumés to demonstrate my thoughts on each section to show you how to do it right. I emphasize the importance of effectively proofreading your résumé, and I list a few common typos I run across when reviewing résumés (sad to say!).

In **Chapter 7**, *Cover Letters*, I address how important cover letters are when applying for a job. I know some hiring managers who don't even look at cover letters, but many do, and if they are interested further in the candidate they'll then look at their résumé. Why take a chance in not providing a cover letter?

In **Chapter 8**, *Stay Positive*, my counsel is to do just that – do not despair. There is no question that this is a difficult time in your life, but staying positive will help you weather this crisis, and may well be the difference between finding a job quickly and having to wait awhile. If you are negative, you may think, "Ah, what's the use?," and back off your job hunt for a few weeks (or months). But – what if the perfect job for you was posted while you took time off to be miserable, and you didn't apply for it? You'll never know, of course, but let that thought work in the back of your mind to spur you on to consistent job search efforts. I even provide a variety of keys to making it through your time of unemployment.

In **Chapter 9**, *Gatekeepers*, I tell you who some of the gatekeepers are – people who have the power to keep you from interviewing with the company or hiring manager – and how to get around them. Gatekeepers include well-meaning secretaries, HR departments. and recruiting software packages.

In Chapter 10, *Before the Interview*, I show you how to prepare for that interview you've finally landed. It includes learning all you can about the company with which you will be interviewing, using your networks to learn more about the company or the hiring manager (and perhaps to even have a good word provided to the hiring manager before the interview), and selecting an "interview suit." The chapter finishes with a section about preparing ahead of time for questions that might be asked during the interview. I let you know how best to sell yourself, how to handle dangerous questions, and how to prepare for and answer those questions you hope never get asked.

In Chapter 11, *The Interview*, I tell you how to thrive during the interview you have worked so hard to get. I introduce the 20-20-20 concept — the first twenty feet, first twenty seconds, and first twenty words – the only time you will have to make a first impression on your hiring manager. Critical things like dressing for success, arriving on time, and learning and using the interviewers' names during the interview are discussed.

I demonstrate that, counter-intuitively, the interview isn't about you – it's about the company. Hiring managers are looking for someone who can help their company, solve a problem, and fit well into their culture and team. Keep that in mind as you interview – what can you offer the hiring manager that will solve his or her problems?

In Chapter 12, *Does Age Matter?*, I address issues associated with age discrimination. My take is that age discrimination is alive and well, and I provide some tactics that might help you be successful in making sure you aren't stereotyped as having issues that other older workers may have. Conversely, I also discuss job-search strategies for younger candidates and candidates without experience.

In Chapter 13, *After You Land Your Job*, I speak about how important it is for you to make a good first impression, that you work hard at your new job, and produce quality work. Topics in this chapter include arriving at work prepared to make a difference, and the fact that your first minutes, hours, days, and weeks you are more or less on probation, as your managers and co-workers and even subordinates are forming their opinions of you, and your work ethic and habits.

In Chapter 14, *Temporary Agencies*, I discuss the value temporary agencies can play in your job search. They provide an employment foot in the door, as companies often turn to temp agencies for support, and end up hiring (or not) the employees who come to them through the temp agencies.

Finally, **in Chapter 15**, *The New Economy & You*, I wrap things up by showing you how much things have changed for job-seekers since the last economic downturn, and show you how you can be successful in this New Economy if you follow the advice in this book that I have specifically tailored to what many are now calling "the new normal" of lower growth and less economic opportunity. Do not lose hope – things can and, as an eternal optimist, I believe will change for the better. But as someone looking for work today you must be prepared for the changes that have taken place in the world of hiring.

If you have discovered job search tactics or strategies that have worked for you let me know. If you have questions – fire me an e-mail and I'll be happy to share a few thoughts with you. And – most important – let me know when you have gotten a job. You may e-mail me at *wdanielquillen@gmail.com.*

Good luck and happy hunting!

3. PLAN TO STAY, PREPARE TO LEAVE

The biggest mistake that you can make is to believe that you are working for somebody else. Job security is gone. The driving force of a career must come from the individual. Remember: Jobs are owned by the company, you own your career! – Earl Nightingale

In 1979, I joined the AT&T family of companies. My twenty-two-year odyssey with them took me through four Bell System companies: Mountain Bell, AT&T, Lucent Technologies and Avaya. It was a wonderful environment to learn important business lessons – they had the money to do things right. During my last ten years in that AT&T family of companies I worked as a Human Resources professional in several organizations, including Avaya Labs (formerly Bell Labs).

I remember well a day in the mid-1990s when I was attending a meeting with AT&T's Executive Vice President (EVP) of Human Resources. During the course of his comments he said something that struck me and has remained with me all these years. Speaking of our careers, he said that as employees we should *"plan to stay, prepare to leave."*

I have to be honest — I was shocked to hear those words from one of the senior executives of my company. Wasn't this one of those companies you started work for as a youth and from which you retired thirty-plus years later? I must admit I was a little put off initially – sure seemed a funny thing to say, and one that didn't exactly engender company loyalty in the hearts and minds of his listeners.

However, over time I have come to see the wisdom of that comment. It was said at a time when the economy was robust and the company was doing well. Perhaps my EVP saw difficulties looming on the financial horizon. Regardless, the more I thought about what he said, the more it made perfect sense to me. About this same time, I attended a conference taught by famous author and motivational speaker Stephen R. Covey. His counsel was that our résumés needed to be fresh and updated at all times. He said we should be actively working to gain new experiences and education to enhance our résumés. He stressed that if our résumé is the same today as it was six months ago, we were in trouble.

Let's explore both halves of my EVP's statement: *Plan to stay* and *Prepare to leave*.

PLAN TO STAY

If you are currently out of work, you may be tempted to skip this short section. But I encourage you not to do so. While you may now be out of work, the things I will share will help you once you do secure a job.

When he said we should plan to stay, I don't believe my EVP was speaking about warming a seat at the company because we had a pulse and were still contributing at least somewhat positively to the bottom line of the company. I think he meant we should continue to be an important element of whatever organization we are a part of. I think he meant we should compete for new positions – laterals or promotions – that would allow us to continue to contribute to the organization and expand our career horizons.

One of the key ways to remain with an employer is to make yourself and your contributions important to the company. By saying this, I am not implying that you should become secretive about what you do, to jealously guard the processes and procedures you follow so that no one else would know what to do if you left. I have seen that technique time and time again, and I have yet to see it work. What happens, quite frankly, is that you are viewed by the organization as a road blocker rather than a bridge builder, and when it comes time to thin an organization, road blockers are often among the first to go.

What I mean when I say you should make your contributions important to the company is this: you should become the best at what you do. Are you one of many electrical engineers at your company? Then become the best electrical engineer the company has. Always meet your deadlines, in fact, bring your projects in early whenever possible. Always complete your projects at or under budget. Make sure they are flawless in their design and delivery. Check and double-check your work. Then check it again. The product you present should be without error.

For his entire life, one of my children has had a genuine intellectual curiosity. While his siblings wanted to watch cartoons on Saturday mornings, he preferred watching the *Discovery Channel,* and learning about things like the sand-trap spider of the Sahara. You would do well to apply the same intellectual curiosity to your job. Gain all the knowledge, certifications, and education you can. Keep current with developments in your field. Most fields have newsletters, magazines and/or websites that discuss the latest innovations and thoughts in your employment universe. Be up to speed on them, and explore any you don't understand.

All of us have a job description of one sort or another, whether formal or informal. I have made a career out of working in the areas I call the "white space" – the activities and projects that need to be done that fall between job descriptions. My boss needs a volunteer to work on XYZ project? I'm her man. Corporate

Be intellectually curious

needs input on ABC proposal? I am happy to provide it. Doing this not only makes me more important to the organization, it also allows me to gain new knowledge and insights into the way the company operates, allows me to develop and expand my networks, etc.

As you make yourself valuable to your organization, it is important to keep in mind that no one – and I mean no one – is indispensable to an organization. You may be important, you may be hard to replace, but if you leave – for whatever reason – the company will most likely continue without you. I once heard Steve Jobs – co-founder of Apple Computers – describe how nine years after he co-founded Apple, he was forced out as their CEO and left the company. While he returned a dozen years later to his Apple CEO post, the important message here is that no one is indispensable.

Don't get so locked into one career path that you become expendable when the company decides to close down that area of the business. If you have a variety of skills and knowledge applicable to the company, if your department or position has been identified for downsizing or elimination, you may be able to find another position within the company. However, if you have only one area of expertise, you may find yourself leaving the company, even though you are a top performer. In this New Economy, even more so than in the old economy, good people hit the streets through no fault of their own.

Early in my career I worked for AT&T in Salt Lake City. One day my boss called me into his office. He said, "Dan, do you want to be a Technical Consultant for the company for the rest of your career?" I said no. He said, "Well, if you want to progress, you're going to have to leave Salt Lake City. To progress in Salt Lake City, either I will have to die or retire, and frankly, I am not planning on doing either for a long time." He went on to strongly recommend that I look for opportunities in Denver, where AT&T's regional headquarters were, or New Jersey, where corporate headquarters were. He strongly recommended the latter over Denver. He said in addition to gaining new job knowledge and skills, probably the most valuable insights I would gain would be how the company operated – how things got done, how products were developed, manufactured, and delivered.

After discussions with my wife, we decided to take the leap, and soon I had accepted a position in Corporate Marketing at the company's headquarters in Basking Ridge, New Jersey. My former boss was correct: I learned invaluable information about how large corporations work. I also expanded my network many times over.

After about four years in New Jersey, a position for which I was qualified opened up in Colorado and I accepted it, moving my family back out west. A few years after that I received a promotion to a new position, and one of the reasons I received the promotion was because of the experience and knowledge I had gained during my stint in New Jersey. However, less than a year later, the company decided they had too many people at my mid-management level in the company, and company-wide cut those positions. Mine was one of the positions targeted for elimination.

But because of the networks I had built in New Jersey, as well as the knowledge I gained through my work there, I was able to find another position within the company.

You must take charge of your career. Over the years, I have heard too many employees grouse about their limited promotional opportunities, the fact that their boss wasn't helping them get promoted, etc. *You* are responsible for *your* career – not your boss! Certainly, he or she can be a valuable resource and tool for you, but at the end of the day, you are responsible for your career. When my Salt Lake City boss had his discussion with me, he merely shared his wisdom and recommendation. I was the one who sought out jobs for which I was qualified. I was the one who made the appointments and went to the interviews.

I understand it's not always possible to pull up stakes and move your family across the country for a job. However, there are always opportunities around for growth and progress. If there is a position you think you would like one day, talk to the individual in the position and learn about it – the skills and knowledge required to be successful. Have an exploratory interview with the supervisor of that position. Let him or her know you would be interested in applying for the position if it ever came open, and you'd like to find out more about how you could prepare yourself to be a strong candidate. I can't imagine a manager not being willing to allow such an interview – and believe me, he or she will remember you when the job comes open.

Once you identify the gap between your skills and knowledge and those required to qualify for the new position, lay out a plan to get the skills, knowledge and experience. If certain certifications are required, perhaps your company has a tuition reimbursement program that will allow you to get the certification on the company's dime. And even if not, don't be afraid to invest a little in yourself. Perhaps you can volunteer to work on projects with one of the individuals currently in the position, to learn and gain some knowledge and experience. Perhaps there are projects in your own organization that will allow you to gain experience and skills that you can point to should you be fortunate enough to interview for the position.

As I mentioned earlier regarding my son, be intellectually curious. And then lay out a plan to get the skills, knowledge and experience you lack so that you can be a viable candidate when the position does come open. Your boss may be a valuable ally in this effort – he or she can pave the way for you to take classes, get involved in projects that will give you necessary experience, etc. But again, your career progression is not your boss's responsibility. Be prepared to recommend and request opportunities.

As a final thought, let me share something that has bothered me for years. In every organization I have been in during my professional life, there are individuals who seem to take joy in throwing rocks at the organization. They are vocally critical of the company, its processes and procedures, etc. Every opportunity they get to have an audience they express their negative opinions. In speaking with these individuals through the years, they invariably see themselves as crusaders – representing the Voice of the People to management. Often, however, these Champions of the Downtrodden find themselves the first that are let go during downsizing, and they often wonder why. If you recognize yourself in this paragraph, my word to you is: *change*. Knock it off. Few beyond a close group of associates like, much less approve of, your cynicism and negativity. In recent years, my HR mantra has been: "Sometimes the squeaky wheel….gets replaced."

> Sometimes the squeaky wheel … gets replaced

In short – plan to stay with your current employer by doing the things that will make you invaluable to your employer.

PREPARE TO LEAVE!
Now on to the second part of my EVP's slogan: *Prepare to Leave*. You must prepare yourself for the eventuality that you may one day leave your company. They may merge with another company, making your job redundant with other high performers in the combined company. The economy may worsen – as we've seen – and to survive, your company may need to have significant layoffs. The possibilities of things that may cause you to lose your job are endless, and the time to prepare is *now*, not when you receive your RIF (Reduction in Force) package!

Many years ago when I was in college, I interviewed for a position more or less on a lark. I figured the worst that could happen was that I would gain interviewing experience. But even though I had a little over two years left to complete my degree, the company offered me a job with a starting salary over twice what I would have made had I completed school and went into the profession for which I was studying. As I had just gotten engaged, it was not a difficult decision for me to leave school. I did so with the promise to myself that I would finish my degree by going to night school.

Several job transfers and six years later, my boss called me into his office. Here's how our conversation went:

> Phil: "Dan, you don't have your degree."
> Me: "No, I don't. But I have been working on it a bit through the years."
> Phil: "How many credit hours are you away from your degree?"
> Me: "About 70."
> Phil: "Dan, you are at a point in your career that not having a degree will hurt you. You *have* to get serious about it and finish it."

Phil was absolutely correct. That conversation provided the impetus for me to complete my degree in about 18 months from the time of our discussion. I attended classes, I tested out of courses and I studied online (actually, this was before online classes – I took correspondence courses). Phil's conversation was some one of the best professional counsel I ever received, and I understood that I *had* to act on it.

A few years later I began noticing that most of the jobs in our intra-company jobs database said, "Bachelors degree required, Masters degree preferred." I decided I ought to get my Masters degree.

I took the GMAT test and scored well enough to get into the schools I was considering. But the timing just wasn't right. Work was busy. My family was young and growing – we had just had our sixth child and our oldest was nearly a teenager. I was busy at church. So I put off the decision to begin.

Over the next several years I seriously considered jumping into an MBA program, but again, the timing just didn't feel right. Then one day I had a serious talk with myself. I decided the time would *never* be right – if I didn't make this a priority, it would continually get left on the back burner. In essence, here's the conversation I had with myself:

> "Dan, if this is important to you, then just bite the bullet and do it. If it's not, then quit considering it and move on."

When faced with that challenge, I decided to get my MBA. I would be less than honest if I told you it was easy. The class work wasn't bad – it's amazing how much you pick up over the years of running a household, working for a Fortune 20 company, etc. But it was difficult juggling the time commitments. About half-way through the program I was sorely tempted to quit, but decided to persevere. I hung on and completed my MBA – again, one of the best professional decisions I ever made.

And – this is almost the best part – my company paid for the completion of both my Bachelors and Masters degrees through tuition reimbursement! Although I may not have realized it at the time, I was truly preparing to leave AT&T by making myself more marketable to other employers.

And why do I share this information to many who may not have a job today? The point is that in the New Economy most well-paying jobs require you to have at minimum a Bachelors Degree, and many prefer or even require a Masters Degree. If you are out of work, this is a great time to go back to school and finish your degree, or get an advanced degree. Many of my colleagues have gone back to school in an effort to reinvent themselves, earning degrees in fields they had not worked in before in an effort to get work in another industry or role.

Many colleges today are geared toward adult learners, individuals who need to start or complete degrees around the demands of full-time jobs and their families. Night classes, online classes, weekend classes, etc. are all part of their curriculum.

But what about money? It's sort of difficult to pay for tuition and expenses out of unemployment funds and/or savings. There are many options – student loans, grants, scholarships. Entire books have been written on those topics, and your local college or university will be able to assist you in navigating those waters.

In 2009, my son (the intellectually curious one) graduated from Gonzaga Law School. He had received a job offer, but it was rescinded, so he was looking at graduating without a job – a somewhat unheard of situation in the legal community prior to 2009.

But 2009 and 2010 proved to be the toughest on record for law school graduates. Law schools that were accustomed to having 95% of their graduating classes find employment as attorneys within six months of graduation were now seeing those numbers drop to 30% to 50%.

My son and I discussed that if the recession kept him from finding a job as an attorney, he might just as well ride out the recession by getting his LLM (Master of Laws) – another advanced degree for attorneys. As it turned out, the firm that originally offered him a job and then rescinded it came through with another offer and he began his career there.

How sad I am when I review résumés of people who are seeking a professional position, but don't have a college degree – what a difference it makes. Go get an education! If you are unemployed and do not have your degree —start (or finish) – your education. Get certifications. Learn new skills. Increase your value to potential employers. In this New Economy, I frequently see candidates with Bachelors and Masters degrees applying for even entry-level positions. It's tough to compete without a degree. And while it may not seem fair, education is one of the first elements companies will use to screen a candidate pool from hundreds down to a more manageable number. Those without degrees simply aren't considered. Even if you are the most qualified person for the job, you run the risk of not having your résumé even make it to the desk of the hiring manager. However, don't be overly dismayed — I'll share tactics that may get your résumé reviewed even though it gets screened out early in the process!

What am I doing
to prepare to leave?

4. SOCIAL NETWORKING

The leverage and influence social media gives citizens are rapidly spreading into the business world. — Simon Mainwaring

In today's economy, job hunters need to use every tool available to them in their job hunt, and that includes social networking.

For those of you over 45-50, you may not be too familiar with using social media networking in your job hunt. That's where I come in – I'll share a few thoughts about social networking — the things you ought to know and consider as you seek to end your unemployment by utilizing yet another tool in your job-hunting arsenal. If you're under 45 or so, you most likely know the deal: Facebook, LinkedIn, and other social media have become quite important in all walks of life and business – including the business of searching for a job!

While there are many tools to assist you in your social networking, the three primary ones today are LinkedIn, Facebook and Twitter. Each deserves a few moments' consideration as tools to assist you in your job search. I'll address each one in order, based on their usefulness in networking. From a usefulness perspective, I prioritize them as:

1. LinkedIn
2. Facebook
3. Twitter.

LINKEDIN
LinkedIn (www.linkedin.com) is a massive organization topping 200 million participants, many of whom may be able to assist you in finding

work (it's just finding the right one!). In addition to being a place where you can have an online resume / presence, you can also connect to friends, colleagues, customers, etc. Those connections, and individuals connected to them, may provide opportunities for you to bring an end to your employment search.

Once you set up a LinkedIn account, you go about identifying people you want to include in your network. Use the *Search* box on the homepage to do this. The *Search* box has a drop-down box that provides several search options, including *People, Companies,* and *Jobs.* You can search for people by their name, or you can search for them in your own company – or former companies – if you're just getting started.

Once you identify individuals with whom you would like to connect, simply click on their name, and you'll be able to click a *Connect* button, which will send a message to them asking them to connect to you. Then, all they have to do is accept your invitation, and *voila!,* you are connected.

Once you are a member of LinkedIn (there is no cost to join the basic level), you can search companies in which you are interested to see if you have any connections at those outfits. If you do, you can reach out to them to let them know you are interested in a job at their company, and perhaps you can get an introduction to the hiring manager, or perhaps they will agree to carry your résumé to the hiring manager with a good word.

So – let me show you how that might work. Let's say you are very excited – you submitted a résumé to IBM for a position that would be a perfect match for you. About half an hour ago, an internal recruiter from IBM called you to tell you the hiring manager had reviewed your résumé and would like to interview with you. Calmly, you say yes, that would be fine. You work with the recruiter and set a time and place for the interview.

As soon as you hang up, your first thought is: "Who do I know at IBM?" The answer is a little disconcerting – you know no one – or at least no one that you are aware of. What to do?

Then you recall all the people with whom you are connected through LinkedIn. You go to the LinkedIn website and start poking around. From the navigation bar on your home page, you click on *Interests*. A drop-down box with three options appears:

- Companies
- Groups
- Influencers

You click on *Companies*, and you're taken to a page that has a *Search* box; you type in IBM, hoping that you find someone you know who works there. You click on the *Search* icon, and suddenly the pictures of five people appear. You recognize two of them immediately – one goes to church with you and the other was a former college roommate. Both of them are noted as 1st-degree connections – meaning you either accepted their invitation to connect, or they accepted your invitation. This is exciting – there are two people whom you know well who may be able to provide some positive input to the hiring manager with whom you are interviewing. You reach out to them (either via a message though LinkedIn, their personal e-mail address, or possibly even a phone call), explain about your upcoming interview, and see if one of them knows the hiring manager. Even if neither of them knows the hiring manager (IBM is a large company), one or both of them may be willing to provide a positive reference for you.

Next, you turn your attention to the other three people, all listed as 2nd-degree connections. A 2nd-degree connection is connected to someone with whom you share a 1st-degree connection. None of these second-degree connections looks familiar. You click on the picture of the first one, and you see that he is connected to a woman you worked with a few years earlier. While this 2nd-degree connection doesn't know you, he does know your former coworker, and he might be willing to let the hiring manager know what a great guy your former colleague thinks you are. So you reach out to her, let her know what you need – a positive reference – and she agrees. You ask her to reach out to the fellow who is her 1st-degree contact (your 2nd-degree), and again, she agrees. Things are looking pretty good for you.

You check out the other two individuals listed as 2nd-degree connections, and the people they know that are connected to you aren't as close to you, and would probably not be able to provide much of a reference for you.

Even though you're excited about the interview with IBM, you know you need to keep searching for work. Back on your LinkedIn homepage, on the navigation bar, you see a tab for *Jobs*, and you select it. In the *Search* box that appears, you can type in a search string: *Accounting New York, Medical sales Phoenix*, etc. When the jobs come up, they will also tell you how many people in your network work at that company. Clicking on that notification lists all those individuals, and where they are in your network. It will let you know if any of your connections are connected to the hiring manager, which provides a great opportunity for you.

I want to share another very powerful way to use LinkedIn in your job search. When you first lose your job, LinkedIn provides an awesome opportunity to get the word out that you are searching for work, the kind of work you are seeking, and your qualifications to work in that field. To let your network know you are out of work, do the following:

From your LinkedIn homepage, there is a text box adjacent to your picture. (The text box will be next to your picture *if* you have posted a picture of yourself. If not – you should. Make certain it is a professional-looking picture.) You can place a message of up to 600 characters in that box. For example, here's a message you might post if you were a teacher looking for a position:

> Greetings! I am reaching out to my LinkedIn network to tell you that I am leaving Buffalo Trail elementary. Enrollment is down, and only 3 1st-grade teachers will remain. Since I have been there the shortest time, I am odd woman out. I have a degree in Elementary Ed from CU-Boulder, and have taught 1st grade for 7 years. I love teaching these budding scholars, and hope to continue to do so in the southern Denver metro area. I am good at what I do; I have received 3 Teacher of the Quarter awards from the PTO in the last 5 years! If you know of any 1st or 2nd grade openings, please let me know!

Once you have entered your text in the box, select whether you want it to go to your LinkedIn network (it will go to your 1st-, 2nd- and 3rd-degree connections), LinkedIn + Twitter (remember — only the first 140 characters will post to Twitter), or just to your 1st-degree connections (select *Connections*).

To illustrate the power of this post: as of this writing, I have 538 connections. As soon as I post a message, 538 of my closest friends will be notified that I have posted the message. AND all their connections – my 2nd-degree connections. AND all their connections (my 3rd-degree connections). I have no idea how many 1st-, 2nd-, and 3rd-degree connections I have, but it must number in the thousands, if not tens of thousands. I didn't want to go through all 538 of my connections to see how many 1st-degree connections they had (my 2nd-degree connections) – that would be too time-consuming. But I decided to take a sample: I looked at the first ten of my connections listed. Of those ten connections, there were 3,992 1st-degree connections, an average of 399 connections per person…sort of. Individuals with more than 500 connections only list "500+ connections" (and five of the ten connections I checked had more than 500 connections). So, I have at least 3,992 connections from those ten individuals. If all 538 of my connections average 399 1st-degree connections in their networks, then as soon as I post a message, 214,662 individuals receive notification of my message – and that's only my 1st- and 2nd- degree connections. Add the 3rd-degree connections, and the number is unimaginably large! That is part of the power of using LinkedIn in your job hunt.

As you explore LinkedIn, I think you'll quickly see how valuable and powerful it can be in your networking, and it will amaze you how quickly your network will build with just a little effort on your part.

In addition to connections in LinkedIn, a valuable opportunity exists by joining groups aligned to your skills / career. Sales, nursing, accounting, construction, legal, etc., and about any career you can imagine has a discussion group. Join them – they offer you the opportunity to meet and connect with other people in your profession or industry. Participate in the discussion groups – remember, though, that your responses are accessible to everyone in the group, so be circumspect in what you say. Have knowledge about a question or problem someone in the group has? Then offer your assistance. Weigh in. Have a good question that others might be able to answer? Then by all means post it. It was by participating in an industry discussion group that I learned of a number of job openings, and interviewed for one of them.

Of the three social networking sites covered in this chapter, LinkedIn gets my vote as the most valuable for networking while looking for a job.

FACEBOOK

As mentioned earlier, I think LinkedIn far outperforms Facebook and Twitter as a job-hunting tool. But Facebook has its advantages, too. Consider your Facebook "friends" – here are potentially several hundred (or more) individuals – family members, colleagues, friends and acquaintances, who may be ready networkers for you. A word on Facebook about your loss of employment and request for assistance may result in a lot of activity, including the possibility of obtaining work. In fact, I am aware of a number of friends who put the word out on Facebook and within a very short time they had found employment, based on the input and information from their friends.

Here's how it works on Facebook. Let's say I post essentially the same announcement I shared as an example in the LinkedIn section:

> Greetings! I am reaching out to my Facebook friends to tell you I am leaving Buffalo Trail elementary. Enrollment is down, and only 3 1st-grade teachers will remain. Since I have been there the shortest time, I am odd woman out. I have a degree in Elementary Ed from CU-Boulder, and have taught 1st grade for 7 years. I love teaching these budding scholars, and hope to continue to do so in the southern Denver metro area. I am good at what I do; I have received 3 Teacher of the Quarter awards from the PTO in the last 5 years! If you know of any 1st or 2nd grade openings, please let me know!

Remember – LinkedIn is limited to 600 characters, so I had to be somewhat economical with my words there. But on Facebook, I know of no limit (other than people's willingness to read pages and pages of comments!), but you should probably keep your message somewhat short and sweet.

I have 400 friends on Facebook. The moment I post this above message, those 400 people will learn about my job search. Also, with any luck, one or more of them will be aware of an open position – perhaps at a child's school, or through friendship with a principal, or any number of ways.

But – you can also expand your Facebook network, similar to what was done in LinkedIn, although not quite as automatic or as dramatic. Once you post your comment ("What's on your mind?") on Facebook, ask all your friends to *Share* your post. If they will do that, it will exponentially multiply the number of people who are seeing your post and know you are looking for work – a good deal! However, it's not automatic as it is in LinkedIn, and my experience is that few Facebook friends – certainly nowhere near 100% — will share your post. Some will, and perhaps many will, but not 100%.

Frankly, the reason I ranked Facebook above Twitter as far as usefulness is because of the job-searching *danger* that exists through Facebook accounts. Recruiters and hiring managers routinely check the Facebook accounts of individuals applying for jobs. If they see you doing or saying stupid things on Facebook, you may miss out on employment opportunities. If you *must* include your wild side to the world, do it through a pseudonym.

In addition, in recent years, press coverage has revealed well-publicized incidents that resulted in people being fired because of things they posted on Facebook. In one case, it was information critical of the management of the person's company, and in another, an individual revealed information about a new product that was under development by his company. Both times, the courts upheld the firings. So be warned, and be careful.

TWITTER

Twitter is a social networking phenomenon that has risen in importance in recent years. It's a way of sharing short, quick bites of information – tweets – with friends and colleagues (tweeple). Since Twitter limits messages to 140 characters, you don't have to worry about people going on and on. Some might be tempted to dismiss Twitter because of the brevity of the messaging. After all, how much important information can just a few characters provide?

Careful on Facebook!

If you are among those who question the value of short messages, consider the following:

"I only regret that I have but one life to give for my country." Nathan Hale (74 characters)

"Give me liberty or give me death." Patrick Henry (48 characters)

"That's one small step for man, one giant leap for mankind," Neil Armstrong (74 characters)

"Never was so much owed by so many to so few." Winston Churchill (62 characters)

As well as the following:

"I am not a crook." Richard M. Nixon (35 characters)

"I did not have sexual relations with that woman." William Jefferson Clinton (66 characters)

"Read my lips – no new taxes." George H. W. Bush (47 characters)

"A crude and disgusting video sparked outrage throughout the Muslim world." Barack Hussein Obama (95 characters)

So now that you are convinced that 140 characters can convey powerful messaging – for good or ill – let's talk a little more about Twitter as a tool in your job search arsenal.

As with LinkedIn and Facebook, you have the opportunity to add many individuals – friends, colleagues, vendors, etc., to your job-search network. You can let your *Lists* (your Twitter network) know that you are out of work, what kind of job you are seeking, or about an upcoming interview with a company.

Using the example I used in the LinkedIn and Facebook sections, if I sent the exact same message, it would be:

Greetings! I am reaching out to my Twitter List to tell you I am leaving Buffalo Trail elementary. Enrollment is down, and only 3 1st-grade

Hmmm – that's probably not the most efficient message to send via Twitter. It needs to be tweaked (tweeped?) quite a bit; something more like:

> Looking for 1ˢᵗ grde teacher job. 7 yrs exp. PTOs Teacher of qrtr 3 times. Prefer SW Denver area. Love to teach little ones. Can u help?

Quite a different (written) message, although most of the critical points are included. (Her being laid off because of low enrollment isn't in this message…that can be shared in a subsequent tweet if she felt it was important for her tweeple to know.)

Let me provide a short contextual tutorial on Twitter vocabulary, since it's a little different than what you might be used to in Facebook and LinkedIn.

Here you go:

English	Facebook	LinkedIn	Twitter
Message	Status Update	Status	Tweet
People in network	Friends	Connections	Lists
Someone you follow	Friends	Connections	Friend
Someone who follows you	Friends	Connections	Follower
Forwarding a message	Share	Share	Retweet
Private message	Message	Send a Message	Direct Message (DM)
Subject line:	—	—	hashtag (#)

That last item in the table may require a bit of explanation. Remember, Twitter limits users (tweeple) to 140 characters. A definite Twitter shorthand has evolved to allow tweeple to maximize those 140 characters. So instead of saying:

> Looking for 1ˢᵗ grde teacher job. 7 yrs exp. PTOs Teacher of qrtr 3 times. Prefer SW Denver area. Love to teach little ones. Can u help?

Perhaps you say:

> #jobsearch – 1ˢᵗ grde teach. 7 yrs exp. PTOs Teach of qrtr 3 X. Pref SW Dnvr. Lve 2 teach little 1s. Can u help?

And that leaves me an extra 28 characters to wax eloquent (elqnt).

Seriously – the hashtag (pound sign to some of us — #) tells your followers the title of your topic.

So why Twitter instead of Facebook and LinkedIn? Or in addition to? There are some fundamental differences between these three social networking platforms. We've mentioned the obvious: the 140-character limit on Twitter is pretty…limiting. Facebook has no maximum (I have Friends that go on and on…and on), and LinkedIn has a 600-character limit.

Beyond that – to follow someone in Facebook and LinkedIn, you must *Friend* them or request a *Connection*. If the person you have made such a request to does not respond…you're not in their network and you cannot follow them (unless someone in your network is in their network and shares their comment). While Facebook and LinkedIn are private parties, Twitter is more like a Mosh Pit – all comers welcome and allowed! You do not have to be accepted by someone to follow them. Think about a famous person-ality who keeps her fans abreast of her latest activities – she doesn't have to accept 8,432,000 Friend requests – she can just send a tweet out, and all those who are following her will receive it. Or – in a job-search scenario – perhaps you follow several recruiters in your industry, or follow a number of companies who use Twitter. In recent years, more and more recruiters and companies are using Twitter to get the word out about jobs.

One of your job-search Twitter goals should be: **Retweeting**. As with Facebook and LinkedIn, Twitter users have their networks – lists. As you post information about your unemployment and and job search, you hope your list of followers will retweet (share) your tweet with their lists – thus multiplying the number of people who know about your job search and may be in a position to assist you.

As with Facebook and LinkedIn, individuals can respond to you – if you are a follower of the sender, then the process is a Direct Message (DM); if you are not a follower of the sender, they can still reach you by sending a public message (called @Reply). You'll get the message, but so will your list of tweeple.

One of the strengths of Twitter is its real-time aspects. LinkedIn and Facebook are somewhat real-time, but Twitter is as real-time as it gets. News about events worldwide are flashed over Twitter. That means you may be able to get the inside track on jobs that are posted – if you are on Twitter. Recruiters and internal company recruiters are beginning to use Twitter more and more – they post jobs on Twitter to targeted groups of candidates. If you are not on Twitter, you may be left out and never even learn about the availability of jobs for which you are qualified.

As you can see, this social networking is more than just for *social* networking; perhaps it could be called *Employment* networking!

Use social networking in my job search!

5. WHAT DO YOU DO NOW?
FIRST STEPS AFTER A LAYOFF

A man cannot be comfortable without his own approval. – Mark Twain

Many years ago when I was early in my corporate career, I transferred with AT&T from Salt Lake City, Utah to Basking Ridge, New Jersey (talk about a culture shock!). My department was on half of one floor, and another department was on the other half. A few weeks after I arrived, the employees of the other department were summoned to a 5:00pm, mandatory all-hands meeting. They were all informed they were losing their jobs and they had sixty days to find a new one.

Even though it wasn't my organization, it felt like a blow to my mid-section. I had just moved my family 2,200 miles across country. I knew no one. All my networks were back in Utah. What would I do if that happened to me and my organization? What would I do?

I mulled and worried about that for several weeks. Then one day as I was driving home thinking about it, the thought occurred to me: "If it happens to you, you'll go out and get another job. You're good at what you do, you have a good skill set and experience. You'll be fine." And that was it – I ceased worrying about it.

And so it will be with you. If you are one of the 20,000,000+ Americans currently out of work, you will get another job. It may be difficult, but you will beat this. You're good, you have good experience, and you'll find work. One of the most important tools you'll have in your job search arsenal is your attitude. Do whatever it takes to be positive. But also realize that in today's New Economy, you may be looking for awhile, so prepare to be in this for the long haul. At the same time, don't dawdle in getting your résumé out there.

I adopted the attitude that the very next job for which I applied would be *The One* that ended my unemployment. That meant I had to work hard, and not let any grass grow under my job-hunting feet. I'll admit that was easier to do in the first days and weeks of my unemployment, but it got more difficult as time went on. But – continue reading and you'll learn tactics that will assist you in getting through those job-hunt doldrums.

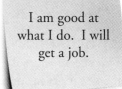

I am good at what I do. I will get a job.

Understand that with this New Economy, good people are hitting the streets at a record rate. Economists estimate that 20,000,000 Americans are out of work, and many more are severely under-employed. And – economists will tell you that the real unemployment number is probably closer to 15% to 17%. Several years ago the government changed the way they calculate unemployment, and the real number is much higher than reported. And these higher levels of unemployed feel real to me, based on the number of my friends and acquaintances who are out of work. At the time, my LinkedIn network had just over 500 individuals in it. Recently I received an e-mail from LinkedIn telling me that 101 of my associates changed jobs during the previous year – 20%. I scanned the list, and while some had changed voluntarily, the vast majority had changed involuntarily. Perhaps you have had a similar experience.

So — cut yourself some slack, straighten your back and stand tall. You lost your job, *not your pride.*

So, what steps should you take to begin your job search? Read on and I'll tell you.

RÉSUMÉ

A good résumé is critical to your job search. It should highlight your experience, skills, abilities and accomplishments. It should be squeaky clean – no typos, grammar difficulties, etc. But there's oh so much more – and that's why I have devoted an entire chapter to creating a résumé that will present the most positive you. More on that later.

COVER LETTER
Equally as critical as your résumé, I believe, is a good cover letter. This element in your job search tool kit is so important I have provided a chapter for that also.

GET ORGANIZED
As you begin your job search, take time to organize your efforts. I can be a bit obsessive in my organization, and find that structuring my search helps me keep my mind uncluttered and on track.

The first thing I did was create a spreadsheet for my job hunt. It kept me focused, helped me plan my work and follow up. Initially the spreadsheet had only a few columns:

• date
• name of Company
• title of position

Over time, I expanded the columns to contain the following list of headings:

• date
• interviews
• name of Company
• job board where job was found / referred by
• title of position
• salary range
• contact
• comments
• login / password
• website address

Some of the headings are self explanatory (date, job title, etc.), but here's just a word or two on several of the others:

Interviews
As I mentioned, I am obsessive about some things. I was interested in tracking my success – or lack thereof. So I created a column that tracked interviews. Whenever I got an interview with a company, I put a 1 in that column. At the end of the spreadsheet I had a *total* column, so I could tell

at a glance how many interviews I was getting. I only included an interview once for a company, even though I might have had several interviews at the company. I was more interested in how many companies I interviewed with, not the total number of interviews within a company. For example, I had seven interviews with 26 people at one company! But I only counted it as one interview in my spreadsheet.

There was more to this column than mere counting. It gave me an opportunity to see if there was a pattern developing – was I more successful in getting interviews for positions that had a particular title, from a particular job board, etc.

Job board where job was found / referred by
I was interested in seeing which job boards yielded the best results. I also wanted to know who had referred me to a particular company.

I ended up adding another tab on the spreadsheet listing all the job boards I was searching, with the numbers of jobs I found and interviews I received through each job board / referral. More detail on that later in this chapter.

Salary range
I found this was an area I was interested in tracking. Sometimes applications software required you to insert your salary expectations, and this was a helpful category. It was also helpful to know in case I got into salary negotiations.

Contact
I used this column to put the name and contact information for people important to this particular job – the person who referred me, hiring manager's name, recruiter's name, people with whom I interviewed at the company, etc.

Comments
I found I needed to make comments about who I had spoken with, what they said, etc. A typical entry was:

> 8/14 — Heard from Susie Recruiter today at Acme Company. She wanted to set up an interview for 8/19.
> 8/19 – Interviewed with Harry Hiring Manager today. Felt the

interview went well, wished I had researched the company a little more before the interview."

Login / password

As you'll learn later in this book, as you progress in your job search you will run into applications software. Many of them require logins and passwords. Unfortunately there are a half dozen variations (at least!) of what they will and will not accept as logins / passwords. Some required your e-mail address as a login, while others wouldn't accept that. Some required passwords to be eight characters long and required a non-alpha character: ?, !, *, etc. In a very short amount of time I realized I couldn't keep track of all the variations I had used, so resorted to adding a column in my spreadsheet to capture the information.

Website address

When I found a job for which I was interested in applying, I cut and pasted the web address in this column. That way if I had questions later on about the position, I could go there with ease.

An important note on that last item: many of the jobs I applied for didn't yield interviews until five, six, eight weeks after my submission. Invariably, by the time I was contacted for an interview, job ads had expired and I couldn't find a copy of the job description any longer. So when I was called for an interview, I couldn't review the job description to plan my interview attack. I learned this very early in my job search, so added a tab in my spreadsheet titled *Job Descriptions*. I cut and pasted each job description into this worksheet. I included a column with the company's name and listed the jobs alphabetically by company so it was easy to find later.

NETWORKS

Although this is a difficult time in your life, this is not the time to keep to yourself. Tell everyone you know that you lost your job and are looking for another. This may be one of the most important moves you make as you begin your job search.

Earlier I mentioned I hadn't searched for a job since 1979. Actually, my exact words were: "The last time I had to *actively* look for a job as an external candidate was in 1979." But in 2001, I was working with Avaya. To my amazement, they offered an early retirement package that was too good to pass up, so I prepared to take the leap.

Shortly thereafter, I was speaking with a group of friends at church. I indicated I would be leaving Avaya in about three weeks, and was looking for work as a Human Resource professional.

A week later I received a call from one of the men with whom I had been speaking:

> Troy: "Dan, didn't you say you were looking for a job?"
>
> Me: "Absolutely."
>
> Troy: "And what did you say you did?"
>
> Me: "I do Human Resources."
>
> Troy: "That's what I thought. The Director of Human Resources at my law firm just announced he was leaving. Is that something you'd be interested in?"
>
> Me: "Yes indeed. I would love to work for your firm, and I have the experience to do that job."

He agreed to contact the hiring manager about me and see if she would accept my résumé. A day or two later he called back to say she would accept my résumé.

I interviewed a few days later and was offered the job. The job offer was extended a few days prior to my early retirement from Avaya. I was leaving Avaya on a Wednesday. I could have started at the firm on Thursday, but decided I wanted to be retired for awhile, so set my start date on the Monday following my retirement. (By the way – I really enjoyed my short-lived retirement – all two days of it. I am looking forward to the time when I can be retired for an extended period of time!)

After I started with the firm, I asked the hiring manager why she had hired me. She said, "Well, your résumé was a good one, and you had good experience. But had Troy not recommended you, I would not have invited you in for an interview because you had no law firm experience. But we trust Troy, and his recommendation swayed us to decide to interview you."

And with that, I began a wonderful ten-year career with a large law firm – all because a member of my network remembered I was looking for a job and put in a good word for me.

Here's what I recommend: Identify all your friends and acquaintances who may be in a position to know of jobs that might be available. Let them know you are looking for a job, and what your skills and experience are.

Years later, when my stint at the law firm ended, here's what I did first:

In addition to my LinkedIn network, I went through the address book in my e-mail and Facebook, and identified another two hundred individuals. Among them were friends, neighbors, former work acquaintances (including a number at my former firm), fellow church members, vendors who had called on me, etc. I developed an e-mail list with all their e-mail addresses, then I sent them the following e-mail:

> Subject: A little assistance please!
>
> Greetings,
>
> As some of you may know, the law firm I have been at for the past decade has outsourced my role, so I am actively seeking a position at another firm or company. You are receiving this e-mail because you are someone I know and trust, and I am hoping you will assist me. As you know, most positions in today's work environment are gotten through networking. It occurred to me that all of you know far more people and have many more contacts in companies than I could ever possibly have, and that's where I need your assistance. Periodically, I will send you a list of companies to which I have applied. Applying to companies today is generally through a faceless website that then scrubs your résumé for key words. If you have the right key words, and the right number of them, your résumé is forwarded to the hiring manager. If you do not have the specific key words, even though you may be the best qualified

applicant, your résumé may never be forwarded to a hiring manager.

And that's where you come in. If you know someone at one of the companies at which I have applied, a kind word to your contact on my behalf might enable my résumé to reach them — or they might be willing to call my résumé to the attention of the hiring manager. Or — even though they have my résumé, it may be in a stack of hundreds of résumés. Your support might be just the motivation for the hiring manager to seek and review my résumé, especially if you attach my résumé for them to review (I have attached my résumé for your review and forwarding if you feel it appropriate). I promise future e-mails will be much shorter, consisting mainly of the list of companies to which I have recently applied.

Even though you have my résumé, let me share a few highlights:
— I am seeking a senior HR position (Director or VP)
— I have 20 years of progressively more responsible HR experience
— I have an MBA
— I am SPHR certified (sort of like a CPA designation for accountants)

If you have questions, please ask away. You may contact me at wdanielquillen@gmail.com or 303-555-1212.

Thanks for your assistance and consideration!

Daniel Quillen

Responses were immediate from many of those to whom I sent the e-mail. I received many well wishes, and more than a few job leads from that initial e-mail. What's more, I now had 450 people in the business world keeping their eyes open for positions that might be appropriate for me.

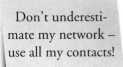

Don't underestimate my network — use all my contacts!

A recruiter friend of mine feels so strongly about how effective networking can be that he tells his candidates: "Your net*work* is your net *worth*."

JOB SEARCH WEBSITES

An invaluable tool for your job search will be job search websites. I place them in the following categories:

- Career category websites (e.g., HR, engineering, teaching, government, graphic arts, etc.)
- Industry-specific websites
- General websites
- Aggregators
- Specific company websites

Let's look at each of these briefly:

Career Category

Most professions I know of have job websites specific to their industry or profession. In my case, as an HR professional, I identified a number of websites that focused on jobs in the Human Resources field. These included:

- Andrew Hudson's job list
- Colorado Human Resources Association
- SHRM

Industry-specific websites

My most recent ten years of HR experience was in the legal industry, so I made certain I included several websites that represented law firms. I used one national website and several local websites. If you are not aware of websites specific to your industry, there are several ways you can discover them. The first is to Google them. Go to the Google *Search* box and type: *(your industry) job websites*. Also, ask industry colleagues which websites they would recommend.

General Websites

We've all heard of one of the premier general websites available out there: Monster.com. I have to admit that for years, I was not a big fan of Monster.com, feeling it was too big and too general to be of use to me, either as an employer or as a job candidate. But I was pleasantly surprised at the value it provided during my job hunt. Here are some other general websites you might consider:

- Careerbuilder.com
- Craigslist.com
- Jobing.com

Aggregator Websites
There are a number of excellent websites out there that I term as aggregators. They scan industry, company, and industry-specific websites for job openings, then pull the openings they find across the web onto their website. So it's sort of one-stop shopping for job seekers. One of the best I found was Indeed.com. Here's a short list of aggregator websites I can recommend:

- Diversityjobs.com
- Flipdog.com
- Indeed.com
- Jobs2careers.com
- Juju.com
- Justjobs.com
- Simplyhired.com
- TopUSAjobs.com (subscription)
- Vast.com
- Yakaz.com
- Ziprecruiter.com

Specific Company Websites
Is there a company in your community for whom you would like to work? How about one of the *Top 50* or *100 Companies to Work for in America*? Many of those very popular companies don't bother placing job openings any place but on their own website. I identified companies in my community I wanted to work with, and routinely checked their websites for openings for which I was qualified.

A word about subscription job search websites. First of all – be cautious not to over-extend yourself – you are after all, in a situation where you need to guard your resources closely. I was intrigued by TheLadders.com, a job search website which only posts positions with salaries over $100,000. My initial thought was that I really couldn't afford to be signing up for websites that charge when there are so many out there that are free. I mentioned this to a friend of mine who had recently been involved in an extensive job search. He said to me, "Dan, you're looking for a job that pays over

$100,000. Don't you think $20 or $25 per month is a pretty decent investment?" When viewed from that perspective, I decided he was right, and I subscribed.

My success by website / source
Earlier in this chapter I promised to share the results of my job search – the number of jobs found and interviews I received by job board / networking referral. Here's the synopsis:

Source	Job Leads	# Interviews	% interviews / jobs
Andrew Hudson	4	0	0%
Career Builder	11	1	6%
Colorado HR Association	18	2	11%
Company websites	13	0	0%
Execunet	2	0	0%
Ladders	21	5	24%
LDSjobs.org	13	8	62%
LinkedIn	4	1	25%
Monster.com	7	4	57%
National Association of Legal Administrators	3	0	0%
Networking	17	8	47%
Recruiters	7	2	29%
Society of Human Resource Managers	4	0	0%
Indeed.com	6	0	0%
Totals	130	31	23.85%

Here are a few quick notes about some of the above websites:

Career specialty or industry websites
Several of the websites above were specific to my HR career (SHRM, Colorado Human Resources Association, Andrew Hudson) or industry (National Association of Legal Administrators).

Recruiters
Occasionally I was either contacted by recruiters or found a job ad they had placed.

Company websites
Company websites were those of companies I thought would be great to work for, so decided to check their websites on a regular basis. Companies in this category included IBM, Google, Microsoft, etc. As you can see, my efforts in this area yielded poor interview results (0 interviews), even though I found 13 jobs that matched my qualifications (10% of the jobs I submitted on). Regardless, if I were starting out a job search again, I would still check these websites.

Networking
This category represents those jobs and interviews I got through the efforts of my network. You can see why I suggest networking so strongly – 13% of the jobs for which I submitted came through this source, and I was successful in getting an interview 47% of the time.

LinkedIn
LinkedIn proved to be a good, although not prolific, source for me. I joined a number of discussion groups for HR professionals. Occasionally another HR professional would post an opening in those discussion groups, such as: "I am seeking candidates for a Director of HR position at my company. Anyone interested should forward me their résumé through LinkedIn."

I immediately had a contact within that company with whom to speak, so this was a great option for me.

LDSjobs.org
This is a website sponsored by my Church. In addition to a rich source of jobs (10% of the jobs I submitted on) and a high percentage of those leads turning into interviews (62%), they had an employment center that offered classes on interviewing, résumés, etc. They were a valuable resource for me in my job search. Their services are available to individuals who are not members of the LDS Church. Contact the local Employment Center of the Church of Jesus Christ of Latter-day Saints to learn more.

Recruiters / Headhunters
I am often asked my opinion on recruiters / headhunters. My opinion is: use them. Seek them out. Let them help you find a job. But – do not just provide your name to a few headhunters and sit back and wait for your phone to ring. View them as one of many arrows in your job search quiver.

Headhunters typically focus on one industry – for example, I am personally acquainted with recruiters that focus on legal, healthcare, government, accounting, IT, etc. If, like me, your profession is one that can be practiced in multiple industries, then look for headhunters in a variety of industries.

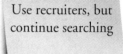

Understand that each recruiter you deal with may be representing many – dozens or even hundreds of – candidates (depending on the firm size). I had a recruiter contact me about a position during my job hunt. We talked about

Use recruiters, but continue searching

my résumé, and he felt I might well be a match for one of the companies he was representing. He sent me the job description, and asked me to provide him with a few lines about my skills in the main areas the job description identified. He wanted to provide the company with a synopsis of my HR career. After reviewing the job description, I determined the company was seeking an HR Professional with the following skills and experience:

• Benefits
• Diversity / EEO
• Training
• Expatriate Management and Relocation

I decided to make it easy on my headhunter; remember – he probably represented many other candidates – I wanted to enable him to represent me well. After reading the job description, I provided him with a thorough review of my experience as it related to each of those areas.

My recruiter professed to being "bowled over" by the completeness of my synopsis, and said it would be a great assist to him as he represented me to the company.

Recruiters are just like many of us in the New Economy today – busy and probably doing the work that two or three others had done previously. If you can make the job easier for recruiters, they will be more likely to work hard to place you.

SET A SCHEDULE
Okay, you have garnered all the tools at your disposal for your job hunt:

résumé, cover letter, networks of friends and associates, job search websites, and perhaps even a few headhunters. What next?

Your job, my friend, is to find a job. You must treat it as you would the job you just left – you should put in at least 40 hours a week job hunting.

"What?!" You may ask. "How can I possibly job hunt 40 hours a week?"

Well, the answer is simple. If you are doing it right, I believe you'll find that 40 hours each week will be barely enough to do all you need to do. Following is a sample week's job-search schedule that worked for me:

Monday
8:00am to 11:00am – Search job websites, apply for any jobs that are of interest.

11:00am to noon – research companies you are interested in / have applied to. Try to find the hiring manager at the company. Company websites, calls to HR departments, networking contacts, etc. can all help with this.

Noon to 1:00pm – Lunch

1:00pm to 5:00pm – work your network – contact members of your network via e-mail or telephone. See if they know anyone at the companies where you have applied.

Tuesday
8:00am to 9:00am – research companies you are interested in / have applied to. Try to find the hiring manager at the company. Company websites, calls to HR departments, networking contacts, etc. can all help with this.

9:00am to noon – Search job websites, apply for any jobs that are of interest.

Noon to 1:00pm — Lunch

1:00pm to 5:00pm – work your network – contact members of your network via e-mail or telephone. See if they know anyone at the companies where you have applied.

Wednesday
8:00am to 10:00am – work your network – contact members of your network via e-mail or telephone. See if they know anyone at the companies where you have applied.

10:00am to 11:00am — research companies you are interested in / have applied to. Try to find the hiring manager at the company. Company websites, calls to HR departments, networking contacts, etc. can all help with this.

11:00am to noon – Search job websites, apply for any jobs that are of interest.

Noon to 1:00pm — Lunch

1:00pm to 5:00pm — Search job websites, apply for any jobs that are of interest.

Thursday
8:00am to 11:00am – Search job websites, apply for any jobs that are of interest.

11:00am to noon – research companies you are interested in / have applied to. Try to find the hiring manager at the company. Company websites, calls to HR departments, networking contacts, etc. can all help with this.

Noon to 1:00pm – Lunch

1:00pm to 5:00pm – work your network – contact members of your network via e-mail or telephone. See if they know anyone at the companies where you have applied.

Friday
8:00am to 9:00am – research companies you are interested in / have applied to. Try to find the hiring manager at the company. Company websites, calls to HR departments, networking contacts, etc. can all help with this.

9:00am to noon – Search job websites, apply for any jobs that are of interest.

WHAT DO YOU DO NOW?

Noon to 1:00pm — Lunch

1:00pm to 5:00pm – work your network – contact members of your network. See if they know anyone at the companies where you have applied.

By following this schedule, you'll put in a minimum of 40 hours each week. Some days may be a little shorter, while others will be longer.

You may be one of those people who prefer to have the same schedule each day. If that's the case, by all means, do it that way: set yourself a schedule and follow it every day, day in and day out. I found that altering the schedule kept it interesting to me, and I didn't get into a rut.

Print your schedule and post it, especially if you are doing your job-hunt activities at different times each day. If you are doing the same schedule each day, you needn't print and your schedule if you can remember it.

With any luck at all, you will only have to follow your schedule for a very short time.

NETWORKING GROUPS

I found networking groups to be valuable to me in my job search. I joined several. One of them was a group of businessmen who belonged to my church. The first Tuesday of each month, about sixty of us met at a restaurant in the Denver metro area for lunch. Before lunch began, each of us stood and introduced ourselves. In the group were employers as well as those seeking employment. My introduction was simple and to the point:

> "Hi, my name is Dan Quillen. I was recently laid off from my position as the Director of Human Resources at one of the largest law firms in Colorado. I have nearly 20 years of progressively more responsible Human Resources experience. I also have an MBA and am SPHR certified – sort of a CPA for Human Resources professionals. I am seeking a position as a Director or Vice President of Human Resources."

Others in the group introduced themselves with the name of their company and the position they held there. Frequently, one of those individuals would finish by saying, "Dan (or Tom, Bill, Sam, etc.) – my company has an opening you might be interested in – let's talk after lunch." I got a number of leads and a few interviews through this networking group.

I joined two other networking groups – an "Over 50" group sponsored jointly by two of the counties in the south Denver metro area, and one my church sponsored. The former met on a monthly basis and had speakers come and speak on various topics, and provided networking opportunities among the group. That group consisted 100% of job seekers, so it wasn't as good a networking opportunity as the previous group I mentioned.

The group sponsored by my church was a valuable resource for me: they offered a résumé class, a job interviewing class, and a job search class that shared various resources for job seekers.

It would be well worth your time to seek out and join networking groups, both those consisting primarily of job seekers as well as those consisting of a mix of job seekers and employed individuals.

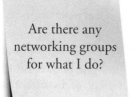

Are there any networking groups for what I do?

STAY BUSY

While most books about how to get a job will contain information about résumés, interviews, etc., I believe this bit of advice may not be found in any other job-finding book. I could be wrong, but think not.

Stay busy. You are going from working probably 50 hours a week (including commute time) to perhaps 40 per week. That leaves you time to do other things. Here were some of the things I did and didn't do during the months I was job hunting:

Things not to do:
No daytime TV! I know myself, and know I can be a bit of a couch potato. I like old movies and a number of older TV shows: *Bonanza, Gunsmoke, Everybody Loves Raymond, Seinfeld*, etc. Because I knew it would be a temptation and a great time waster, I decided I would not watch any TV until 5:00pm.

Not only do I write books, but I like to read them — books are my friends. So I decided not to read any books between 8:00am and 5:00pm.

Things to Do

Cultivate new skills. For our entire married life, my wife was almost always the family cook. Even after she began working full-time, that was a role she continued to fulfill. Sure, I would "cook" dinner now and then – usually grilling steaks, pork chops, ordering pizza, etc., but those times were few and far between. I decided it wasn't fair for me to be home all day while my wife worked and then expect her to come home and cook dinner for me. So I found her recipe book and started my cooking career. I started with casseroles that were family favorites, then got gradually more adventurous, finally culminating in a gourmet meal of Cornish game hen and skirlie (a Scottish dish)! It was a lot of fun, and it helped make me feel more productive and contributing to the household.

In addition to cooking, I assumed many other household duties – vacuuming, doing the laundry, and grocery shopping. These were done after (or sometimes during – like laundry) my "work" day. They did not take the place of my job search – that always took priority – but they helped fill the rest of the hours in my 50-hour work week.

One of the best things I did was begin and continue an exercise program. Exercise is an excellent stress release, and I am sorry to tell you, but you are likely to experience stress during your time of unemployment.

Keeping busy will help you stay positive, and not sit around brooding or fretting about your situation. As you make and keep yourself busy doing productive things, you'll find the days do not drag, you'll be able to stay focused on your job search, and you'll feel productive. Depression is something you must constantly guard against.

Here is an important thought about keeping busy: *Keep your pipeline full of résumés and applications.* My job search lasted five and a half months. I soon noticed a pattern in my job hunt: most job interviews I received were either within two to three days of my submission, or five to six weeks after my submission. If you take a week off beginning today, you may notice a week to ten days without an interview five or six weeks from now.

Prior to my unemployment I had arranged to visit an out of-town daughter and her family. Since the trip was already paid for, I opted to continue with it.

However, it wasn't a vacation — I loaded all my information – résumé, résumé template, cover letter template, job search matrix, etc. on a laptop and headed for Chicago. Even though I was out of town, I wasn't on vacation. I still carved out significant portions of the day to conduct my job search. While there, in fact, I was contacted by a recruiter as well as set up several interviews.

So – keep that pipeline filled.

UNEMPLOYMENT BENEFITS

Some of the best advice I got from several of my unemployed friends was to begin the process of registering for unemployment as soon as possible. The process for each state is different, but one general observation is it can take up to six to eight weeks to begin receiving unemployment benefits after you register. Each state has a formula they use to determine the amount of benefits you may receive. Beware – it will come nowhere near replacing your former salary. Its intent is to allow you to keep body and soul together and allow those out of work to meet basic needs. As of this writing, following are the maximum weekly / monthly unemployment payments you can expect from various states:

State	Weekly	Monthly
Alabama	$265	$1,060
Arizona	$241	$964
California	$450	$1,800
Colorado	$454	$1,816
Connecticut	$555	$2,220
Delaware	$330	$1,320
Florida	$275	$1,100
Georgia	$330	$1,320
Hawaii	$560	$2,240
Iowa	$459	$1,836
Kansas	$420	$1,680
Louisiana	$258	$1,032
Massachusetts	$674	$2,696
Mississippi	$230	$920
Montana	$446	$1,784
New Jersey	$600	$2,400
New Mexico	$455	$1,820

State	Weekly	Monthly
New York	$405	$1,620
North Dakota	$470	$1,880
Rhode Island	$566	$2,264
Texas	$426	$1,704
Utah	$451	$1,804
Washington	$604	$2,416
Wyoming	$387	$1,752

I have not listed all the states – I just wanted to list a representative cross-section so you could get a flavor for what various states offer. If your state isn't listed, just Google *maximum (state name) unemployment benefits*.

I can make neither heads nor tails from these numbers. One might think that a state that has a high cost of living would also provide high unemployment benefits. In some cases that's true (Massachusetts — $674 per week, the most in the US), but in other cases, it's not (New York — $405 per week.). Conversely, you would expect states with much lower costs of living to pay less in unemployment benefits. Makes sense, right? Then explain to me why Kansas and North Dakota both pay more per month than New York. While the funds are a mix of state and federal funds and employment tax from corporations, each state has the ability to determine how much they will pay their residents. It's a conundrum to me, to be sure. It won't help to move, either. You receive unemployment benefits from the state where you worked, not the state you move to.

It is important to remember the benefits shown in the chart above are maximum benefits – your benefits may be lower based on how much you earned while working. Each state also has specific residency requirements, quarters worked where you earned income, etc. In general, most states pay unemployment benefits of about 40% to 50% of your average weekly wages up to the state's maximum unemployment amount.

Generally speaking, unemployment benefits last twenty-six weeks. As of this writing, after you exhaust your state's maximum number of weeks of unemployment benefits (normally twenty-six weeks), you may be eligible for federal unemployment payments.

As of this writing, there are four tiers of federal unemployment benefits available. The first tier provides up to fourteen weeks of benefits and is available in all states. Tiers 2 through 4 depend on the unemployment rate of your state. At worst, you'll get fourteen weeks of federal unemployment benefits, and best case, you'll get forty-seven extra weeks of unemployment benefits beyond your state unemployment benefits.

As of this writing, the maximum weeks of unemployment (state plus federal) is 73 weeks.

Finally, remember to weave through the labyrinth you'll find for registering for unemployment benefits as soon as you can.

HOUSING

As soon as you learn of your job loss, you should advise your mortgage company about your situation, and see if there is anything they will do to assist you. Foreclosures are bad for individuals and families, but they are also bad for mortgage companies. Often, they will work with you to revise your payment, postpone payments for a period of time (three to six months), etc. The sooner you check with them, the sooner you'll know what options are available to you.

6. RÉSUMÉS

The will to win, the desire to succeed, the urge to reach your full potential...
these are the keys that will unlock the door to personal excellence.
— *Confucius*

Since this is a book on getting a job, you know there will be a chapter on résumés. I have reviewed tens of thousands of résumés during my career. I have screened them for my own hires, as well as for other hiring managers.

As I have reviewed résumés, one thing has been painfully clear – too many people do not spend enough time on theirs, and it costs them the job. Yet this could be your most important job-search task. There are other important elements to your job hunt, but many of them will not be able to be used if you don't get in the door, and your résumé is one of the primary ways you'll open that all-important door.

Some experts say you have less than thirty seconds to grab a résumé reviewer's attention with your résumé. Personally, I spend more like the following time reviewing résumés:

• first review = 3 to 5 seconds;
• second review (if you pass the first review) = 15 seconds.

That may seem difficult to believe, but experienced résumé reviewers – like HR departments or managers who hire frequently – can determine in a moment or two whether or not they are interested in the candidate.

Now, I am going to share with you a method to craft your résumé that should increase your potential to land interviews (and a job!) **by 300% to 500%** over what your chances will be if you don't follow my recommendations.

When I was searching for a job after my layoff in mid-2011, I submitted 130 applications. Those 130 applications yielded 31 job interviews for me – nearly a 24% hit rate. Having been out of the job searching business for many years, that seemed pretty anemic to me. However, as I spoke with other job seekers and met with networking groups, they were all amazed at my level of success. Leaders of the networks of which I was a member claimed their group was averaging more like 3% to 5% hit rates, and they all wondered how I was achieving such a high success rate with my résumé. They asked that I present classes on what *magic* I had that made my résumés more appealing and successful. Those presentations eventually led to the writing of this book.

In this chapter I have shared several copies of my résumé for your review. Next, I will discuss general information that you should know about résumés, and then I will show you each segment of my résumé and provide thoughts and comments about it.

Here's the first version:

W. Daniel Quillen, SPHR
My Address, Centennial, CO 80015 303-555-1212
wdanielquillen@gmail.com

SUMMARY OF QUALIFICATIONS
Senior Human Resource professional with a record of documented achievement and measurable performance in various industries. Strategic leader committed to providing best-in-class Human Resources support. Seasoned leader with impeccable ethics and integrity. Strengths include:

• Legal Compliance	• Employee Relations	• Benefits Expertise
• Organizational Design	• Recruiting	• Employee Development
• Multi-site HR	• Interpersonal skills	• Evaluations

PROFESSIONAL EXPERIENCE
Director of Human Resources   2001 to Present
Holme Roberts & Owen LLP, Denver, CO

– Protected the firm from lawsuits by handling all disciplinary actions up to and including terminations using sound employment law practices. Over the course of ten years and 200+ terminations, there were no lawsuits filed against the firm for employment actions.

– Used competency modeling expertise to assess required skills for positions, and identified skill gaps within the work force. Training curricula developed to address deficiencies within the various work groups, resulting in a more efficient and skilled work force.

– Developed, launched and administered a voluntary staff development program designed to enhance staff skills and enrich their work experience. Ongoing classes supported and attended by over 90% of staff. Hailed as a significant success by firm management.

– Effectively managed all health benefits for the firm. From 2006 through 2011, negotiated over $2,000,000 in savings for the firm while maintaining one of the best benefits packages in our market (excellent benefits, low deductibles, moderate premiums, etc.).

– Implemented overtime guidelines that saved the firm over $750,000 over a two-year period while at the same time maintaining high levels of client service. This effort improved per-partner revenues, allowing us to attract and retain partners.

– Skilled at cultural transformation and organizational design. Over the past several years several firm mergers / acquisitions required effective cultural assimilation and organizational design. Efforts resulted in rapid employee and partner assimilation and a more efficient work force.

Director of Legal Recruiting   2005 to 2007
Holme Roberts & Owen LLP, Denver, CO

– Directed the recruiting and hiring of attorneys and paralegals into the firm. Over a two-year period, brought 44 associates and 11 paralegals into the firm. This allowed the firm to increase revenues, lower its per-attorney overhead and increase partner profits.

– Established national contracts with several recruiters, negotiating lower rates than were normally offered. Savings for the firm were substantial, as rates were typically 33% lower than normal.

– When our Director of Legal Recruiting left the firm, was asked to take over her responsibilities while maintaining Director of HR responsibilities until a suitable candidate could be found. Served in dual roles for 18 months, saving the firm over $250,000 in salary expense.

Here's the second version:

W. DANIEL QUILLEN, SPHR

My Address, Centennial, CO 80015
303-555-1212 wdanielquillen@gmail.com

SUMMARY OF QUALIFICATIONS

Senior Human Resource professional with a record of documented achievement and measurable performance in various industries. Strategic leader committed to providing best-in-class Human Resources support. Seasoned leader with impeccable ethics and integrity. Strengths include:

• Legal Compliance	• Employee Relations	• Benefits Expertise
• Organizational Design	• Recruiting	• Employee Development
• Multi-site HR	• Interpersonal skills	• Evaluations

PROFESSIONAL EXPERIENCE

Director of Human Resources   **2001 to Present**
Holme Roberts & Owen LLP, Denver, CO

- Protected the firm from lawsuits by handling all disciplinary actions up to and including terminations using sound employment law practices. Over the course of ten years and 200+ terminations, there were no lawsuits filed against the firm for employment actions.

- Used competency modeling expertise to assess required skills for positions, and identified skill gaps within the work force. Training curricula developed to address deficiencies within the various work groups, resulting in a more efficient and skilled work force.

- Developed, launched and administered a voluntary staff development program designed to enhance staff skills and enrich their work experience. Ongoing classes supported and attended by over 90% of staff. Hailed as a significant success by firm management.

- Effectively managed all health benefits for the firm. From 2006 through 2011, negotiated over $2,000,000 in savings for the firm while maintaining one of the best benefits packages in our market (excellent benefits, low deductibles, moderate premiums, etc.).

- Implemented overtime guidelines that saved the firm over $750,000 over a two-year period while at the same time maintaining high levels of client service. This effort improved per-partner revenues, allowing us to attract and retain partners.

- Skilled at cultural transformation and organizational design. Over the past several years several firm mergers / acquisitions required effective cultural assimilation and organizational design. Efforts resulted in rapid employee and partner assimilation and a more efficient work force.

Director of Legal Recruiting   **2005 to 2007**
Holme Roberts & Owen LLP, Denver, CO

- Directed the recruiting and hiring of attorneys and paralegals into the firm. Over a two-year period, brought 44 associates and 11 paralegals into the firm. This allowed the firm to increase revenues, lower its per-attorney overhead and increase partner profits.

- Established national contracts with several recruiters, negotiating lower rates than were normally offered. Savings for the firm were substantial, as rates were typically 33% lower than normal.

- When our Director of Legal Recruiting left the firm, was asked to take over her responsibilities while maintaining Director of HR responsibilities until a suitable candidate could be found. Served in dual roles for 18 months, saving the firm over $250,000 in salary expense.

Senior Human Resources Manager   **1998 to 2001**
Avaya / Lucent Technologies, Westminster, CO

- Due to success in complex HR situations, was asked to provide HR support to 1,400 Avaya Labs (formerly Bell Labs) scientists, a large department with significant complexity to their HR work (organizational development, recruiting, retention, compensation, etc.).

Earned *Exceeded* and *Far Exceeded* ratings and performance bonuses for work with this group.

- Designed a recruiting strategy for our business unit, aimed at recruiting and selecting only "A" players into our business. Allowed us to bring in more qualified employees, reducing turnover and increasing efficiency. Business unit strategy became the model for corporate-wide recruiting.

- When another senior manager left the company, asked to take over management of the other manager's teams. Managed human resource, finance, operations, IT and public relations teams. Saved the company over $200,000 in salary expenses over a two-year period.

- Designed and implemented an organization-wide learning curriculum for managers. Resulting programs identified competency gaps and provided customized learning curricula for managers. Efforts hailed by company executives as break-through, creative and highly efficient.

Human Resources Generalist   1992 to 1998
Lucent Technologies / AT&T, Greenwood Village, CO

- Certified as a Competency Consultant. Because of success in this area, was asked to work with a small team to introduce competency modeling company-wide, including international locations. Competency modeling used for recruiting, employee development and performance management.

- Identified issues and concerns with the company's tuition assistance program. As a result, was asked to serve as business unit's representative on a small core team responsible for developing and implementing a new tuition assistance program, which served 130,000 employees. Results were more efficient and appropriate use of the company's tuition assistance funds.

AWARDS / HONORS

- *"Dan communicates very well; he knows when to talk and write like an employment lawyer, and when to talk and write like a Director of Human Resources.* " (Written comment in performance review by an employment law partner with whom I worked extensively.)

- Participant in "fast track" program for executives who exhibit extraordinary leadership potential. (Fewer than 2% of AT&T's employees are given this opportunity.)

- Freelance author. Fourteen books and several articles in national magazines published.

- Published article on *Society for Human Resource Management* website: Paralegals & the FLSA.

- Wrote article for *The Colorado Lawyer:* Making Healthcare Insurance Affordable for Your Firm.

EDUCATION

Bachelor of Science in Business Administration, with Marketing minor
Thomas Edison State College (Trenton, New Jersey)

Master of Business Administration, with Human Resource specialization
Concordia University Wisconsin (Mequon, Wisconsin)

CERTIFICATIONS / MEMBERSHIPS

Certified as Senior Professional in Human Resources (SPHR)

Certified as Competency Consultant (McLagan Process)

Long-time member of the Board of Directors for the Mile High Association of Legal Administrators.

I have provided copies of my résumé for three reasons – first, throughout the rest of this chapter, I will use my résumé to illustrate a number of points I wish to make about résumés. Second, please turn back and look at the two versions of my résumé critically. Each résumé is identical – same content, same layout, etc. Without taking the time to review each résumé, without taking the time to read for content, I think you will agree that the second one – the one with the formatting, is the more professional looking of the two, and the one that will have a better chance of standing out among the dozens or hundreds of résumés in the stack sitting on a hiring manager's desk. **See the comparison of the first part of each résumé on pages 68-69.**

The third reason I provided it, by the way, is in case you want to copy the format (not the content or experience, please!) to use in your own résumé. I know there are many formats and layouts for résumés…this is one you might consider. It worked for me. It is nothing more than a compilation of items I have seen in résumés through the years. I'd review a résumé and think, "Hmmm, I like the way he presented this. I think I'll adopt that into my résumé." And so on. So – feel free to use whatever in the formatting and layout appeals to you.

Okay – let's get started. Let's begin with some general comments about résumés.

PROOFREADING

A point I cannot stress forcefully enough: it is absolutely critical that your résumé have no typos and no grammar or tense errors. These can sink a résumé as quickly as many other things. While one typo might be acceptable (we all make mistakes!), by the time I get to the second or third typo in a résumé, I am pretty much done with it. Every job I know of requires attention to detail (okay, maybe you can blur the lines a bit if you are an impressionistic painter), and typos in a résumé are just plain unacceptable to most business people.

Be careful of words that a spell checker *won't* pick up:
• hear / here
• there / their / they're
• its / it's (learn the difference between these two!)
• affect / effect (if you aren't dead certain when to use these two words, don't use either!)
• to / too / two
• stray letters. Did you know that if you leave a letter all by itself in a sentence, spell check doesn't flag it as a spelling error? For example: *The cat was n the barn.*

Watch out for what I call *restructuring errors*. Word processing software is great and allows you to make rapid revisions. But sometimes, you leave "orphan words" in your sentences. For example:

Original sentence:

> I have been responsible for leading a team of highly effective benefits and payroll employees.

Intended revision:

> I led a team of highly effective benefits and payroll employees.

Final version (with orphans included – **bolding added to highlight the orphans**):

> I **have been** led a team of highly effective benefits and payroll employees.

I cannot stress enough that you must read and re-read your résumé, making sure there are no typos, grammar issues, etc. And then, once you have read it several times, read it again! Take your time. If you are a writer, the rule of thumb is to review your completed manuscript seven times before you send it to a publisher. I consider myself a pretty good proofreader, and I am always amazed at how many issues I pick up during readings six and seven – especially toward the end of the manuscript.

After you have done your review, have someone whose opinion you trust review your résumé with a critical eye – "yes" men and women are not helpful. I have found that spouses, significant others, parents and siblings are *not* good reviewers – they love you and don't apply the critical eye you need. If you've done a good job, your reviewer probably won't pick anything up. However, they'll be more likely to notice little things that affect your résumé: spacing that isn't even throughout the résumé, some bullet points use periods and some do not, etc.

One caution – if you ask someone to review your résumé, don't be offended by their recommendations. You don't have to incorporate them if you're not comfortable, but don't be offended – they are trying to help you.

W. Daniel Quillen, SPHR
My Address, Centennial, CO 80015   303-555-1212
wdanielquillen@gmail.com

SUMMARY OF QUALIFICATIONS

Senior Human Resource professional with a record of documented achievement and measurable performance in various industries. Strategic leader committed to providing best-in-class Human Resources support. Seasoned leader with impeccable ethics and integrity. Strengths include:

- Legal Compliance
- Organizational Design
- Multi-site HR

- Employee Relations
- Recruiting
- Interpersonal skills

- Benefits Expertise
- Employee Development
- Evaluations

PROFESSIONAL EXPERIENCE

Director of Human Resources   2001 to Present
Holme Roberts & Owen LLP, Denver, CO

– Protected the firm from lawsuits by handling all disciplinary actions up to and including terminations using sound employment law practices. Over the course of ten years and 200+ terminations, there were no lawsuits filed against the firm for employment actions.

– Used competency modeling expertise to assess required skills for positions, and identified skill gaps within the work force. Training curricula developed to address deficiencies within the various work groups, resulting in a more efficient and skilled work force.

– Developed, launched and administered a voluntary staff development program designed to enhance staff skills and enrich their work experience. Ongoing classes supported and attended by over 90% of staff. Hailed as a significant success by firm management.

– Effectively managed all health benefits for the firm. From 2006 through 2011, negotiated over $2,000,000 in savings for the firm while maintaining one of the best benefits packages in our market (excellent benefits, low deductibles, moderate premiums, etc.).

– Implemented overtime guidelines that saved the firm over $750,000 over a two-year period while at the same time maintaining high levels of client service. This effort improved per-partner revenues, allowing us to attract and retain partners.

– Skilled at cultural transformation and organizational design. Over the past several years several firm mergers / acquisitions required effective cultural assimilation and organizational design. Efforts resulted in rapid employee and partner assimilation and a more efficient work force.

Résumé, First Style

W. DANIEL QUILLEN, SPHR

My Address, Centennial, CO 80015
303-555-1212 wdanielquillen@gmail.com

SUMMARY OF QUALIFICATIONS

Senior Human Resource professional with a record of documented achievement and measurable performance in various industries. Strategic leader committed to providing best-in-class Human Resources support. Seasoned leader with impeccable ethics and integrity. Strengths include:

• Legal Compliance	• Employee Relations	• Benefits Expertise
• Organizational Design	• Recruiting	• Employee Development
• Multi-site HR • Interpersonal skills		• Evaluations

PROFESSIONAL EXPERIENCE

Director of Human Resources   **2001 to Present**
Holme Roberts & Owen LLP, Denver, CO

- Protected the firm from lawsuits by handling all disciplinary actions up to and including terminations using sound employment law practices. Over the course of ten years and 200+ terminations, there were no lawsuits filed against the firm for employment actions.

- Used competency modeling expertise to assess required skills for positions, and identified skill gaps within the work force. Training curricula developed to address deficiencies within the various work groups, resulting in a more efficient and skilled work force.

- Developed, launched and administered a voluntary staff development program designed to enhance staff skills and enrich their work experience. Ongoing classes supported and attended by over 90% of staff. Hailed as a significant success by firm management.

- Effectively managed all health benefits for the firm. From 2006 through 2011, negotiated over $2,000,000 in savings for the firm while maintaining one of the best benefits packages in our market (excellent benefits, low deductibles, moderate premiums, etc.).

- Implemented overtime guidelines that saved the firm over $750,000 over a two-year period while at the same time maintaining high levels of client service. This effort improved per-partner revenues, allowing us to attract and retain partners.

I have reviewed résumés and cover letters for years for many people. About ten years ago I ran into an old high school classmate at a retail store. After we exchanged greetings and caught up with one another, he explained he had lost his career job and was just working at this retailer until he could get back into his field. He said he submitted for many jobs, but was never able to get an interview. When he learned I was in HR, he asked me to review his résumé. I was happy to do so, and I am sad to say, it was a veritable train wreck: typos, grammar and tense difficulties, etc., etc. It was, quite frankly, a horrific résumé — one of the worst I have ever reviewed. I spent hours on it, giving him suggestions, even providing him a draft template for a new résumé.

I sent it off to him and heard nothing. Finally after about two months he contacted me and told me how incredibly offended he had been at my criticism of his résumé (even though I was as gentle as I could be). He said he sulked about it for a long time, then finally came to the realization that I really had his best interests at heart, and finally realized how much he appreciated my review.

So – don't be like my old classmate. Be appreciative of the efforts your reviewers make in your behalf. Be gracious even though you may not agree with their suggestions.

Proofreading hint: I found by personal experience that I am a *terrible* proofreader on screen. I have learned that to be effective in my proofreading, I need to print out a hard copy and review it. I don't understand why; guess that's just one of my (many) quirks!

Proofread carefully!

ACRONYMS AND JARGON

Be cautious in using jargon and acronyms. When I began my career, I was in sales for Mountain Bell Telephone. One of my co-workers received a work order (called a *bluie* by employees because it was on blue paper) indicating that a customer wanted a visit (PV – which stood for Premises Visit) for a business line (a 1FB) on their telephone system (KTS). So, bluie in hand, my co-worker called the customer and said:

"Hi, this is _____ from Mountain Bell, and I have a bluie here that says you need a PV to discuss getting a 1FB on your KTS."

Understandably, the customer had no idea what my work associate was saying!

I share this to help you understand that you must be careful with the acronyms you use in your résumé. If the acronyms you use are common to your industry, you may be okay – a hiring manager is likely to know what you mean. But – a recruiter or human resources person may not. If you are going to be using the acronym once in your résumé, I'd suggest spelling it out. If it will likely appear numerous times in your résumé, then I'd suggest using this format the first time:

Senior Professional in Human Resources (SPHR)

Then you can simply use the acronym throughout the rest of your résumé.

LENGTH

Your résumé must be no more than two pages! As a reviewer, I have no patience for three-page tomes, much less those that are longer than that.

But, you ask, I have been in the work place for twenty or thirty years – how can I possibly do justice to each of my jobs in just two pages? The simple answer is: you can't. But there is also no need to do so. If you are late in your career, as many of us are, don't feel compelled to list every single job you have had since you were 18 years old. Jobs and skills from over 15 years ago are not nearly as relevant as what you have been doing the past five years.

In fact, as you prepare your résumé, I suggest that you highlight more responsibilities in the most recent jobs and fewer as you extend back in your career. The exception is if you had a position several years ago that is a perfect match for the skills and experiences required in the job you are seeking today. If that's the case, then by all means – make sure you highlight those experiences and skills from that job as they relate to the one you are seeking. (You'll note the résumé I shared at the beginning of this chapter is more than two pages...it is more than two pages *in this book*, but in real life, it is two pages exactly!)

FORMATTING

I've a few words about the font size I recommend:

Many hiring managers are Boomers – and their eyesight isn't what it used to be. The font size in your résumé should be no smaller than 12-point font; 13-point font is better, 11-point is terrible.

Many hiring managers are Boomers – and their eyesight isn't what it used to be. The font size in your résumé should be no smaller than 12-point font; 13-point font is better, 11-point is terrible.

Many hiring managers are Boomers – and their eyesight isn't what it used to be. The font size in your résumé should be no smaller than 12-point font; 13-point font is better, 11-point is terrible.

Can you see the difference in those identical sentences? The first is written in 13-point font, the second is 12-point, and the third is 10-point. In an effort to get more information in their résumés (and to get to two pages!), many individuals resort to 11- or even 10-point font, and it is a mistake – it is hard to read, and may get your résumé cast aside rather than stress the eyes of your (potential) hiring manager.

Whenever possible, use 12- or 13-font, never 10 or 11. Generally speaking, I try to use 12-point font for most of the body of my résumé, and 13-point font for my section headings.

As of this writing, Word 2007 and Word 2010 are prevalent in the business world. But – they are not pervasive yet. Many companies continue with older versions of Word, and those versions sometimes have difficulty opening Word 2007 / 2010 documents (those that end in .docx). When you send your résumé, I would not send it in Word 2007 / 2010; I would use either Word 2003 or even PDF. To do that, you:

• Draft your document in Word 2007 / 2010 as you would normally do; If you have already saved it, you'll need to save it again by using the *Save As* command

- When the *Save As* box appears, in the *Save As Type*: window, click on the arrow, and select either *Word 97-2003 document* or *pdf*
- Once you have done that, click on *Save* and you're done.

When I do that, I usually change the name so I can see right off which is the other version: *DQ Résumé (Word 97)* or *DQ Résumé (pdf)*.

I think it is worth the effort to avoid the possibility that your dream job, the one you will get if your résumé is reviewed, is offered by a company that has a version of software that can't open .docx files. Don't make your potential hiring manager e-mail you to ask you to resend your documents in a .doc or other format. If you are one of hundreds of applicants, s/he may not make the effort.

HYPHENS

May I just say a word or two about hyphens? Even though it probably won't matter too much in your résumé since most people don't know how to use hyphens, it will make me feel better.

When two words are used together to modify another word, they should be hyphenated, even if they might not normally be hyphenated. Here's an example:

The movie was first rate.

That was a first-rate movie.

In the first sentence, using those two words without a hyphen is just fine. But in the second sentence, the two together form an adjective that modifies the movie – it was a *first-rate* movie. But wait, in the first sentence we say the movie is first rate – doesn't that phrase modify the movie? Yes, however the rule says you only use the hyphen if it comes *before* the word.

The exception to this rule is if the first word used ends in –ly:

I was responsible for leading a team of *highly effective* benefits employees.

Since words ending with –ly are adverbs, you do not need to use a hyphen with the second word.

Finally, numbers from twenty-one to ninety-nine should be hyphenated (excluding, of course, twenty, thirty, forty, etc.).

As I say, most individuals don't know how to properly use hyphens, so I don't think it will matter if you don't use them correctly in your résumé. However, if you are applying for a position as an English teacher, or any other job where the proper use of English is essential (editors, proofers, etc.), then missing hyphens might be the kiss of death. I always appreciate a candidate who uses hyphens correctly, but I don't consider it a typo when not used.

Thanks. Now I feel better.

FONT STYLE

I prefer to see résumés in Times New Roman rather than Arial or Calibri. Times New Roman seems more business-like, more professional to me. I will admit that a great number of résumés I have reviewed for technical positions (IT professionals, engineers, etc.) seem to either be in Arial or Calibri. They do have a much more…*technical* look than Times New Roman, so I suppose they would be okay for those types of positions.

Having said that, I don't believe using any of those fonts would be a deal killer. You must make certain, however, that whichever font you use does not negatively impact the readability of your résumé. There are some pretty fun and crazy fonts available out there, but I would say that's not how you want to make your résumé stand out. Lucinda Handwriting is pretty cool looking, but I think it is a little more difficult to read than Times New Roman.

PHOTOGRAPHS

I have to admit, through the years I have gotten few résumés with pictures of the applicant attached – I can count the number on one hand, in fact. That's good. Unless you are applying for a job as a model, actor or actress, on-screen television role, etc., you should not attach your photograph.

RÉSUMÉ SECTIONS

Okay – so now we've covered some of the general information about résumés. Now let's review a résumé – mine – and I will comment on each individual section, giving you my thoughts on each.

W. DANIEL QUILLEN, SPHR

My Address, Centennial, CO 80015
303-555-1212 wdanielquillen@gmail.com

Nothing fancy here. I prefer to have my name centered and in larger font than the rest of the résumé. I have seen résumés that have the person's name either left- or right-justified, and those are fine too. You do, however, want balance in your résumé. So try putting your name in all three places and see which you like best, which feels best to you.

There is some debate about whether you should put your address on your résumé. A few years ago my son asked me to review his résumé. He had left his address off, and I suggested he include it. Said he: "But Dad, my college careers office said to leave it off." So he left it off.

A few weeks later, he shared with me that he had received a call from a company to which he had applied, asking for his address – seems they wanted to send him some information about the company. I smiled and graciously acknowledged how interesting that was.

Then a few months later I was making a presentation about résumés to one of the networking groups I belonged to. It was a mixed group, consisting of job seekers and hiring managers. Several of the hiring managers weighed in and said they had dismissed résumés because when they looked at the address, they decided the person wouldn't be willing to make the commute. A rich and valuable discussion ensued among the group members on the topic.

So I leave it to you, dear reader, whether you want to include your address or not. The networking group above was generally divided as to whether it should be included. Both groups thought a PO Box was an acceptable compromise. For the record, I did include my address, but I live more or less central to the metropolitan area where I applied to jobs.

Provide your phone number – whether you provide your home number, your cell number, or both is up to you. I have mixed emotions about that. I list only my home phone because I am just not happy with the overall quality of cell phones. Often there is the omnipresent background static /

noise that interferes with the quality, and dropped calls are still too frequent (can you recall the last time your land line dropped a call?!).

If you provide your home phone number, make sure there is a professional-sounding greeting. We have all heard the cutesy two- or three-year-old child's greeting on home answering messages, and while that delights grandma and grandpa, it doesn't present much of a first impression to potential hiring managers or HR departments. Now I can't imagine anyone would dismiss you as a candidate for that reason, but still it begins the first impression.

I don't believe your greeting needs to be as formal and professional as that which you would have at your office. A more generic family greeting is fine: "Hi! You've reached the Quillen residence. We're unable to answer the phone right now, but if you'll leave your name, number and a message, we'll call you back as soon as we can."

Stay away from greetings like: "*You* called *me* – you know what to do." I am not a big fan of music for the first ten seconds of the recording either.

Bottom line on greetings – remember, you are out of a job, and you wish to present the best first impression possible on all contacts with potential employers.

Always – always – include your e-mail address. Once while I was working in my previous job, I asked a large group of my peers whether they called or e-mailed applicants to set up interviews. I was moderately surprised to learn that about 75% used e-mail and 25% called. Personally, I always prefer e-mail – sometimes calls go unanswered, you leave a message, the applicant calls and misses you, etc. I prefer an e-mail – it's quick, clean, and can be responded to at any time of the day or night.

Here is a strong recommendation regarding your e-mail address: ditch the silly, cutesy, goofy e-mail addresses for your job hunt.

A few years ago my 110-year-old staid and stodgy law firm was advertising for an assistant controller. I received a number of résumés, and narrowed it down to a half dozen. I prepared to send e-mails to the applicants inviting them to come in for an interview, when I ran across this e-mail address of one of the finalists:

One_Hot_Woman@_____.com

Amused, I shared the information with my boss. He laughed and said, "Well, we're not hiring her, but I want to interview her!" We both laughed about it.

As it turned out, we didn't end up interviewing her, as an internal candidate stepped up and we promoted her.

Along those lines, here are a few e-mail addresses I have actually seen on résumés, presumably seeking serious employment:

LazyBrain@_____.com
I_Will_Do_Anything@_____.com
ThePartyAnimal@_____.com

Seriously – I don't know what these people were thinking. E-mail addresses are cheap – they are free! Go get one that is much more professional, even if you only use it for your job search.

Also, be certain you check your e-mail frequently – at least daily, preferably several times throughout the day. Recently, at my current employer, we were filling the position of a benefits administrator. We screened the résumés and identified five individuals we wanted to interview. On a Monday afternoon I sent e-mails to the top five candidates, inviting them in for an interview three days hence – on Thursday. Most of the candidates responded within hours of the request. As the day of the interviews approached, I still hadn't heard from one of the candidates. I reached out again on Wednesday afternoon and offered him an interview slot on either Thursday or Friday. He never responded.

We went forward with our interviews. The last candidate we interviewed was exceptional, so we offered her the position on Thursday afternoon.

On Friday afternoon, the candidate who hadn't responded e-mailed to say he had been away from his e-mail for a few days and would love to interview with us. I had to tell him I was sorry, but the position had already been offered to another candidate. *Don't miss out on interviews because you don't check your e-mail frequently!*

As mentioned earlier, people are busier in the American workplace than they have ever been. Sometimes hiring managers will try to bring candidates in between several meetings or projects that are due, and sometimes short notice of interview opportunities is given. I am embarrassed to say that I have e-mailed candidates hoping they would be available the next day for an interview. If you only check your e-mail once a day, or several times a week, you may very well miss out on a golden opportunity! (Note: I *do* cut them some slack if they are not available the next day!)

Okay, now for the next section:

SUMMARY OF QUALIFICATIONS

Senior Human Resource professional with a record of documented achievement and measurable performance in various industries. Strategic leader committed to providing best-in-class Human Resources support. Seasoned leader with impeccable ethics and integrity. Strengths include:

• Legal Compliance	• Employee Relations	• Benefits Expertise
• Organizational Design	• Recruiting	• Employee Development
• Multi-site HR	• Interpersonal skills	• Evaluations

You'll note I have provided three sentences that summarize what kind of candidate I am:

- seasoned HR professional;
- lots of experience;
- documented achievements with measureable performance;
- have worked in various industries;
- impeccable ethics and integrity.

Tailoring

Now we are getting to the meat of résumé preparation and writing. It is crucial to your success in finding a job in today's New Economy. In fact, I feel so strongly about this that I am going to bold and center it:

You must tailor every résumé for every job for which you apply.

Many who are reading this book are searching for a job for the first time in years. And the job search landscape has changed significantly since the last time you may have searched for a job. Hiring managers are so busy with their day-to-day responsibilities that it is hard for them to slow down and review the hundreds of résumés they receive for every opening. Consequently, they have employed resources they never used before to help them. These sources include applications software designed to automatically screen out the least-qualified candidates (more on this later), Human Resources departments and possibly others like administrative assistants, etc.

The days of having one good, generic résumé for every job are long gone – one size doesn't fit all! You must tailor your résumé for every single job you are seeking.

But how do you do that? There are several very easy steps:

1. Print the job ad.
2. Read it from beginning to end, making mental (or literal) notes about the skills and experience they are seeking.
3. Go back to the beginning and read again, this time circling or highlighting those skills and experiences that are important to the hiring manager – those that are listed in the job description.
4. Now, take the list of highlighted items and make a priority list. You will highlight the Top 9 or 10 skills, knowledge and experience they are seeking.
5. Using the list from item #4, begin tailoring your résumé to fit the job description.

Let me give you an example. Following is the job description for a position for which I applied:

Division Manager of Human Resources – City of Aurora

Summary
Plans, organizes, directs and implements strategies for the city's employment, **compensation, employee benefits** and wellness, **employee relations, training** and **recognition**, and **volunteer** programs.

Primary Duties and Responsibilities
Manages the daily operations of City's Human Resources pro-

grams and directs and provides guidance to the Manager of Service Aurora and Training, Employee Relations Officer, Benefits/HRIS Administrator, Employment and Compensation Administrator and Volunteer Program Coordinator. Manages complex intradepartmental and interdepartmental projects covering a wide range of human resources related issues; mentors, provides direction to and evaluates the performance of assigned professional staff; establishes short and long-range divisional priorities, goals and objectives; provides guidance and support for the completion of complex projects including **executive recruitment** and selection, the City's pay plan and job classification system, personnel policies and procedures, **employee benefits plans**, **collective bargaining process**, **training and development** and **volunteer coordinator programs**; develops and recommends employee and employment policies and programs utilizing the knowledge and expertise of the department's professional human resources staff.

Minimum Qualifications
Education: Bachelor's degree in public administration, human resources management or a related field. Masters degree preferred.

Experience: At least 7 years progressively responsible human resources management experience including at least 4 years supervisory experience with at least 2 years division level managerial experience. An equivalent combination of education, training and experience that demonstrates required knowledge, skills and abilities may be considered.

In the body of the job description, I have **bolded** the following key elements of this job:

- Compensation
- Employee Relations
- Recruiting
- Benefits
- Collective Bargaining
- Recognition
- Training and Development
- Volunteer Programs

Scanning these skills and experiences that seem critical to the hiring manager, I note that I have experience in seven of those areas – all but Volunteer Programs (although I have worked with the Boy Scouts for over twenty years). The seven skills on this list will become seven of the nine bullet points I will have in the *Summary of Qualifications* section of my résumé. I need to find two other bullet points they might find valuable. I decided to use *Legal Compliance*, because most every entity I know needs that, and I am particularly strong in that area. And since I would be responsible for Training and Development, I decided to add a related skill: *Organizational Development.*

I also note with satisfaction that I meet their minimum requirements for the position: a Bachelor's degree in business, and an MBA with specialization in Human Resources. I have nearly twenty years of experience vs. the seven they are requiring. I have managed for over twenty years, well above their requirement for four years management experience.

Again, let me say that if you wish to be successful in finding a job in this difficult New Economy:

You must tailor every résumé for every job for which you apply.

One other tip – I would prioritize the bullet points you use for your *Summary of Qualifications.* From your reading of the job description, decide which are the most important skills the company is seeking. The first three should be in Column #1, and the next two most critical skills should be the first skill listed in each of the other two columns. This part of crafting your résumé is more art than science. Usually the top three to five skills are generally pretty easy to determine.

Also – and this is important – use the company's language! If they use the term *Talent Acquisition* instead of *Recruiting*, you should use *Talent Acquisition*. In a later chapter, we'll address applications software, and you'll see how critical it is to have the right terms in your résumé.

Tailor my résumé for every job!

PROFESSIONAL EXPERIENCE

Director of Human Resources   **2001 to Present**
Holme Roberts & Owen LLP, Denver, CO

- Protected the firm from lawsuits by handling all disciplinary actions up to and including terminations using sound employment law practices. Over the course of ten years and 200+ terminations, there were no lawsuits filed against the firm for employment actions.

- Used competency modeling expertise to assess required skills for positions, and identified skill gaps within the work force. Training curricula developed to address deficiencies within the various work groups, resulting in a more efficient and skilled work force.

- Developed, launched and administered a voluntary staff development program designed to enhance staff skills and enrich their work experience. Ongoing classes supported and attended by over 90% of staff. Hailed as a significant success by firm management.

- Effectively managed all health benefits for the firm. From 2006 through 2011, negotiated over $2,000,000 in savings for the firm while maintaining one of the best benefits packages in our market (excellent benefits, low deductibles, moderate premiums, etc.).

- Implemented overtime guidelines that saved the firm over $750,000 over a two-year period while at the same time maintaining high levels of client service. This effort improved per-partner revenues, allowing us to attract and retain partners.

- Skilled at cultural transformation and organizational design. Over the past several years several firm mergers / acquisitions required effective cultural assimilation and organizational design. Efforts resulted in rapid employee and partner assimilation and a more efficient work force.

The *Professional Experience* section of your résumé should begin with your most recent position and work backwards (look later in the chapter for an exception or two).

Unless you have worked for one of the 800-pound gorillas of Corporate America – IBM, Microsoft, Apple, Google, etc. – your future employer will most likely be interested in your job title, not in the company for which you worked. Therefore, your title should be on the first line, and your company should be on the second line:

Director of Human Resources   2001 to Present
Holme Roberts & Owen LLP, Denver, CO

instead of:

Holme Roberts & Owen LLP, Denver, CO   2001 to Present
Director of Human Resources

Consider whether the company name might set you apart for applications within your industry. Perhaps your company is only a 75-pound chimpanzee in Corporate America, but *is* the 800-pound gorilla in your industry. For example, my 250-attorney, 500-employee law firm was tiny in the Corporate American jungle, but it was one of the largest law firms in the western United States. While I generally led with my title, whenever I was applying for a position within the legal community, I led with my firm name. Compared with the other things we'll discuss in this chapter, this is a minor point, so I wouldn't spend an inordinate amount of time deciding on which way to go, but it's a part of the bigger résumé picture.

Unless you have had a succession of short-term jobs, listing your length of service with a company should be done in years. Anything under two-ish years should include the months:

December 2007 – August 2009

A listing of 2007 – 2009 could be as little as 13 months (December 2007 to January 2009) or as long as 24 months January 2007 to December 2009). Of course, if you have had a series of short-term jobs, you may wish to only list the years.

Each of the bullet points under your *Professional Experience* section should be gleaned from the job description and should *match* the nine bullet points you have in your *Summary of Qualifications* section. This section may not be long enough to have bullet points for every one of the nine skills bullet points, but you should hit most of them, and certainly you should address those you feel are the most critical for this position.

Your goal with your nine bullet points and the bullet points under each of your jobs (in particular your latest job!) is to have whoever is reviewing your résumé say to themselves and others: "Holy cow! This candidate has been doing **exactly** the job we are looking for!" *Don't make them pore over your résumé trying to figure out if something you have done in the past matches what what they are looking for.* Make it *easy* for them and tailor your résumé to exactly what they are looking for.

Here's a caution – you can only do this if you have actually had experience in each of these areas. Don't puff your résumé or exaggerate your accomplishments or activities. That's not honest. But do present your true self in the best possible way!

Another thing that is as important as tailoring your résumé is do all you can to make sure every bullet point for each job **has an accomplishment!** You say you were responsible for recruiting? So? Maybe you were the worst recruiter to ever do the job. Can you think of something that was impressive, some accomplishment you can highlight that shows you weren't just some mediocre performer? Sometimes it's difficult to come up with accomplishments, but you must try.

As an HR professional, some of my major responsibilities are to ensure that my company isn't sued because of poor employment practices (discrimination, unlawful discharge, etc.) and to manage our benefits package. Here are two of the bullet points I used on my résumé to highlight those areas of my responsibility, without accomplishments:

- Protected the firm from lawsuits by handling all disciplinary actions up to and including terminations using sound employment law practices.
- Effectively managed all health benefits for the firm, including plan design, negotiation and determining premiums.

And now here they are with **accomplishments added** (the bolding is for your sake – I did not bold these in my résumé):

- Protected the firm from lawsuits by handling all disciplinary actions up to and including terminations using sound employment law practices. **Over the course of ten years and 200+ terminations, there were no lawsuits filed against the firm for employment actions.**

- Effectively managed all health benefits for the firm, including plan design, negotiation and determining premiums. **From 2006 through 2011, negotiated over $2,000,000 in savings for the firm while maintaining one of the best benefits packages in our market (excellent benefits, low deductibles, moderate premiums, etc.).**

During a number of the job interviews I had, the hiring manager specifically mentioned the accomplishments associated with these two areas of responsibility and asked me to tell them more about how I did that.

Some responsibilities lend themselves more to accomplishment identification. Are you in sales? How did you do? Did you consistently exceed your sales objective, year after year? Were you 150% of quota? Were you given a rough territory and you were able to increase sales by 30% over previous years? Did you earn any salesman of the month / quarter / year awards? Tell your story!

Following is one of the responsibilities for which I had difficulty finding an accomplishment:

- Developed, launched and administered a voluntary staff development program designed to enhance staff skills and enrich their work experience.

That's not a task that lends itself to quantification. However, I was determined to show an accomplishment in each of my areas of responsibility, so here is what I came up with:

- Developed, launched and administered a voluntary staff development program designed to enhance staff skills and enrich their work experience. **Ongoing classes supported and attended by over 90% of staff. Hailed as a significant success by firm management.**

I was able to quantify it – 90% of the staff supported this voluntary program – and that management called it a significant success.

Now is not the time (nor during your job interview) to be modest. You have to toot your own horn a little bit. If you don't – the hiring manager won't know just how good you are. Most people I know don't like braggarts, but you must strike a balance between bragging and not mentioning your strengths and accomplishments due to humility.

As you tailor your résumé, you need to not only identify the nine bullet points at the top of your résumé, but you need to change the experience under each of your jobs – not just the first job. That's possible if you have been in the same industry or type of job for some time. But what if you haven't been? What if you have changed jobs and industries in recent years, or even through the years? Then, I suggest you look for experiences and responsibilities you have had that have used skills that aren't industry-specific. Every job I know of requires great attention to detail. Good judgment is needed in most jobs. Identify experiences you have had that demonstrate great attention to detail and spectacular judgment. Then — point that out in your résumé item, mention that such-and-such a project was completed successfully because of the intense attention to detail you demonstrated.

This may seem like a lot of work. It is. But let me put it this way: You can apply for a job in five to ten minutes using a generic résumé, and never hear back from the company, except perhaps one of their canned responses that says, "Thanks, but no thanks." Or you can spend an hour to ninety minutes sprucing up your résumé and tailoring it to the specific job at hand, and increase your possibility of being interviewed four- or five-fold. The choice is yours…but what else are you doing with your time? What else is demanding your attention during these involuntary days off that are now part of your life? I happen to think tailoring each résumé is a pretty good use of your time during this phase of your life.

And make no mistake about it – this will take effort! But, from personal experience I can tell you that as you get into the swing of things it gets easier. First, it gets easier because you are getting better at identifying the elements from the job postings that need to be highlighted in your résumé. Second, if you follow my next suggestion, it will get even easier.

As I was beginning my job search, it didn't take long for me to realize that many of the job requirements for the jobs I was seeking required the same things: experience in benefits, recruiting, employee relations and recognition, training, organizational development, etc. I found myself writing the same entries under my jobs over and over again, or trying to remember in which previous résumé I had already included a particular skill or experience. I decided to get smart: I created a résumé template. I called it *DQ résumé template*. When I opened the template, it looked like my résumé, except that it eventually grew to five pages. Included in it was a listing of all the "nine bullet points" items I had identified during my job search:

- Recruiting
- Legal compliance
- Evaluations
- International HR
- Problem solver
- Organizational design
- Interpersonal skills
- Influencing skills
- Decision-maker
- Benefits expertise
- Mergers / acquisitions
- Benefits expertise
- Employee relations
- Multi-site HR
- Strategy development
- Succession planning
- Leadership development
- Generalist skills
- Analytical skills
- Communication skills
- COBRA, FMLA, HIPAA
- Performance Management

In addition – every time I ran across a new area for which I needed to develop a bullet point to be used under a particular job (along with accomplishments, of course!), I would develop it and put it in my template. By the end of my job search, I had thirty-five such items. I won't list all thirty-five, but here's a sampling:

- Protected the firm from lawsuits by handling all disciplinary actions up to and including terminations using sound employment law practices. Over the course of ten years and 200+ terminations, no lawsuits were filed against the firm for employment actions.

- Investigated and resolved all employee complaints of hostile work place, gender discrimination, sexual harassment, EEOC claims, etc. Resolved all complaints satisfactorily for the complainant and the firm. During ten-year tenure, not one lawsuit was filed against the firm.

- Frequent changes within the firm required effective employee relations and interpersonal skills. Mergers, acquisitions, and recession-related changes in firm policy and guidelines all required extensive ability to inspire and retain employees. As demonstration of success in these areas, one retiring employee observed, "Dan put the *human* back in Human Resources."

- Led all staff and paralegal recruiting. Sourced, interviewed and hired candidates. Ensured candidates had required skills and cultural fit for the firm. Extremely low turn-over rate among new hires resulted in excellent client service and an efficient and productive work force.

- Effectively managed all health benefits for the firm. From 2006 through 2011, negotiated over $2,000,000 in savings for the firm while maintaining one of the best benefits packages in our market (excellent benefits, low deductibles, moderate premiums, etc.).

- Designed and implemented an organization-wide learning curriculum for managers. Resulting programs identified competency gaps and provided customized learning curricula for managers. Efforts hailed by company executives as break-through, creative and highly efficient.

- Designed a recruiting strategy for our 16,000-employee business unit, aimed at recruiting and selecting only "A" players into our business. Allowed us to bring in more qualified employees, reducing turnover and increasing productivity. Business unit strategy was so successful it served as a model for corporate-wide recruiting.

Note for a moment the first two bullet points. Basically they say the same thing, and I wouldn't use them in the same résumé. However, the second one would be used if the job description said the company was looking specifically for someone who had experience in EEOC issues and complaints. The first one might be used if the job description indicated they were looking for someone with legal compliance background. While the items themselves are only slightly different, I used one or the other based on *what the hiring manager* was seeking.

As I was applying for jobs, tailoring my résumé became easy, because I could just go to my template and select a pre-written item. The wording was already worked out, the accomplishment identified and – I had already scrubbed it for typos. All I had to do was cut and paste the item where it belonged on my résumé.

Again, you ask: "Dan, this is an awful lot of work."

And I reply: "Yep."

There is a very good reason to do this. Remember – you have three to ten seconds to hook the résumé reviewer. By completing your nine bullet points and including experiences that mirror those bullet points, you have a much greater chance of getting a second look, and eventually an interview.

As you proceed through the *Professional Experience* section of my résumé, notice that the number of bullet points I include under my older jobs gets fewer and fewer. This is by design. The most relevant work experience I have, the experience that will be reviewed first by my potential employer, should be included in the first of my jobs he or she comes to. As my experience gets older – especially ten and fifteen years ago – there is far less relevance. Therefore, I provide less information on those positions.

Let me make an important distinction here when it comes to tailoring your résumé. **Do not cut sections of the job ad** and paste them into your résumé. Hiring managers will see that and dismiss your résumé as soon as they recognize what you have done (I would, anyway!). Use your own words to tailor your résumé, not the company's words lifted from their job ad.

One last thought on this section: I began my career in 1979, but you'll note the oldest job I list was from 1992. There are several reasons for this – first, jobs much older than that aren't really relevant to most jobs I am seeking now. Second, I don't want the hiring manager to be able to estimate my age.

Okay, on to the next section:

AWARDS / HONORS

- *"Dan communicates very well; he knows when to talk and write like*

89

an employment lawyer, and when to talk and write like a Director of Human Resources." (Written comment in performance review by an employment law partner with whom I worked extensively.)

- Participant in "fast track" program for executives who exhibit extraordinary leadership potential. (Fewer than 2% of AT&T's employees are given this opportunity.)

- Freelance author. Fourteen books and several articles in national magazines published.

- Published article on *Society for Human Resource Management* website: <u>Paralegals & the FLSA</u>.

- Wrote article for *The Colorado Lawyer:* <u>Making Healthcare Insurance Affordable for Your Firm.</u>

This is a section I strongly recommend. This section helps differentiate you from the crowd. So you were a salesman – there are millions of them in America. Oh – you were *Salesman of the Year* for three years in a row? Earned fifteen *Salesman of the Month* awards during your two years with ABC Company? Tell that story! You can include it in the *Professional Experience* section as one of the bullet points, if you prefer, but I like it pulled out and highlighted in a special section like this. If you have only one such element, then it probably doesn't warrant a separate section; but if you have several, put them here.

Use this section to highlight those activities you did that might be considered above and beyond the call of duty. Perhaps you were selected as your company representative at an important industry conference, or wrote a training manual that was adopted by your industry, or you wrote an article for an industry newsletter or website. You exceeded your sales quota every quarter for the past eight years. All these are activities and accomplishments that you are proud of and set you apart from the unwashed masses. Again, tell your story.

Note the first bullet point from this section. Even though it wasn't exactly an honor, I thought this was something I wanted a hiring manager to know about me, because I thought it spoke volumes about my abilities as a human resource professional. So look beyond the plaques and certificates and include things here that tell the hiring manager you are an accomplished and capable employee.

Now onto your Education section:

EDUCATION

Bachelor of Science in Business Administration, with Marketing minor
Thomas Edison State College (Trenton, New Jersey)

Master of Business Administration, with Human Resource specialization
Concordia University Wisconsin (Mequon, Wisconsin)

As with the *Professional Experience* section, unless you graduated from one of the top-tier schools in the nation – Harvard, Princeton, Stanford, or Yale, for example – lead with and **bold** your degree. Do not include your dates of graduation – that allows a screener to determine your approximate age. Some applications software asks for it, but usually allows you to continue in the application without inputting it. I think it's just a wise practice to exclude that whenever possible.

If you graduated with honors – Summa Cum Laude, Cum Laude, etc., — include that. Similarly, if you had a high GPA – 3.9 or 4.0 – I would suggest you include that.

If you attended a branch of a school, be sure and identify the branch; don't just list University of California, write *University of California Berkeley* or *University of California Los Angeles.*

Sometimes there is no difference in the school campuses, sometimes there is. If there is – perhaps the main campus has a more prestigious reputation than your campus – don't try to pass yourself off as a graduate of the main campus. It's not honest, and a quick reference check or transcript requirement will indicate your dishonesty and may cost you your dream job.

Include the field in which you graduated and any minors or specializations you may have had, especially if they are relevant.

In recent years, I have seen a number of résumés that lead with their education section. My recommendation is not to do that, unless you are seeking a job as an attorney or a doctor. Leading with your education section is pretty standard format in the legal and medical industries (for doctors – not nurses, PAs, etc.).

Also, if you graduated from one of the Top-Tier schools in the nation, you may want to lead with that section on your education.

What do you do if you left school without completing your degree, or are still in school (whether full-time or evenings)? I would show that information, and if you have one, put an estimated graduation date. Here is an example:

Candidate for Bachelor of Science in Business Administration, with Mathematics minor
University of Colorado (Boulder, CO) (estimated graduation date: 6/1/20XX)

If you started college and didn't finish, I would include that:

Candidate for Bachelor of Science in Business Administration, with Mathematics minor
University of Colorado (Boulder, CO) (completed five semesters)

While that last is not as strong as having completed your degree, it is still better than no college at all. And – go back and finish! Even if you have to do it one class at a time, do it!

If you have no college or perhaps only one semester, I would not include an education section in your résumé. Do not put the high school you graduated from – it merely highlights that you didn't go to college. If you are a young person just beginning your career, either before or after you have attended college, see the *Age-Related Topics* chapter for a few hints and tips in this area.

If you have taken classes through your work or other venues, it is okay to add classes you think might be applicable to the position for which you are applying. If you do, limit it to those that are directly relevant. But – don't take up valuable space in your résumé just to include these classes. If, however, you get to the end of your résumé and have space remaining, I think it is fine to include these classes in the *Education* section.

CERTIFICATIONS / MEMBERSHIPS

Certified as Senior Professional in Human Resources (SPHR)

Certified as Competency Consultant (McLagan Process)

Long-time member of the Board of Directors for the Mile High Association of Legal Administrators.

From my experience and observation, this section is somewhat new in the résumé world. However, these days companies are often looking for specific certifications, membership in organizations, etc. This is a good place to highlight those accomplishments / activities. The individual items can be included in the body of your résumé with your job experience if you wish, or you can highlight them here. Depending on the length of your résumé (remember – no more than two pages!), you may even put it both places. This may help round out your résumé and keep it from ending 3/4ths of the way down the second page.

SECTIONS NOT INCLUDED

Objective Statement. I am not a fan of *Objective* statements at the beginning of résumés. Are they wrong? I think not. But I prefer to see that information covered in the cover letter. And – I am always amused at those objectives that say something like: "I am seeking a position in the medical industry to utilize my skills and experience." In and of itself, there's nothing wrong with that, except that the job I have open isn't in the medical industry!

Personal. No offense, but I have absolutely no interest in your hobbies, marital status, volunteer work or other such personal tidbits of information. You were a Division 1A collegiate or professional athlete? I'll admit that's impressive to me, broken-down old athlete that I am. But I would prefer to see information like that in an *Awards / Honors* section, or in your cover letter.

As I was writing this book, I reviewed a professional résumé at work with the following *Personal* section:

Married to Cindy, a ceramic artist and potter. We have two sons, Scott, a biologist and Anthony, a music teacher. My family and I enjoy swimming, biking, hiking, skiing, camping, climbing mountains, golf and most any outdoor activities. We also enjoy cultural experiences including art, music, and travel.

Now I am certain Cindy is a lovely woman, and Scott and Anthony are perfectly delightful children, but none of that is something I have the slightest bit of interest in as a hiring manager. (Note: names in the above paragraph have been changed to protect the innocent!)

The only exception I have run across in my review of thousands of résumés is one fellow's *Personal* section that included the fact that he had led a blind climber up Kilimanjaro and Mt. Everest. Now *that* is something I found impressive!

References Available Upon Request. I wish I had a dollar for every résumé I have reviewed with that superfluous ditty appended at the end of a résumé. That is assumed. I have yet to ask a candidate for their references and had them say, "No, I think not."

IN SUMMARY
A couple of closing thoughts on your résumé:

I know we have taken a lot of time in this chapter discussing your résumé. But it is such an important part of your job search – really the first *visible* aspect thereof. Yes, there is preparation up front – organization, identifying networks, etc. – but this is a most critical step. The *Interview* chapter is pretty extensive too, since that's where you really get to shine and hopefully close the deal. But without a great résumé, you may not even get an interview, even though you are the most qualified candidate. What a tragedy for you as well as for the company who would have hired you.

At the end of the day, you must be comfortable with your résumé. It is your calling card, so to speak, and it must feel right and comfortable to you. I promise not to be offended if you don't take my counsel about formatting, organization of the résumé, etc. But you *must* follow my counsel and tailor your résumé for each position, or you probably don't need to read any further – because you won't be interviewing very often. Seriously!

7. COVER LETTERS –
TO WRITE OR NOT TO WRITE?

"Always remember that you're unique, just like everybody else."
– Anonymous

Yes, you are unique – but you need to stand out from all the other unique job-seekers. To do this, you must include an effective cover letter.

One of the big questions in the job search world is whether you should write a cover letter to accompany your résumé. Some hiring managers like them, in fact, prefer them, while others don't even look at them. As a hiring manager, I generally prefer looking at the résumé and often don't get to the cover letter, although I typically read the cover letter for the top candidates. But some of my peers do just the opposite. They scan the cover letter first, and if it piques their interest, they review the accompanying résumé.

If in fact some hiring managers don't even look at cover letters, why should you take the time to write one, much less tailor it for every position? Let me answer that with a short story:

A few years ago I was screening résumés of attorneys for my law firm. I had identified a half dozen top candidates and brought their résumés to our legal recruiting manager. All but one of the résumés had cover letters. As I handed her the stack of résumés and cover letters, I mentioned that one of them didn't have a cover letter. She said, "Well, if they don't care enough about the job to write a cover letter, then I am not interested in reviewing their résumé." And she didn't.

Not knowing whether the HR department or hiring manager reviews cover letters, do you want to risk losing a $60,000, $90,000 or $100,000+ job for the sake of a one-page letter that would probably take you five minutes to tailor? With my apologies to the writer of the poem *For Want of a Nail*:

For Want of a Cover Letter
For want of a cover letter the interview was lost.
For want of an interview the job was lost.
For want of a job the house was lost.
All for the want of a cover letter.

So, now that you've decided to write a cover letter….

Your cover letter should be as crisp and clean as your résumé. There should be no typos. It should be short – absolutely no more than one page. Length in a cover letter is deadly, as it is in résumés. As with résumés, you have only a few moments to grab a reviewer's interest.

Like your résumé, your cover letter should be tailored to every position for which you apply. Tailoring your cover letter isn't as extensive a process as the process for tailoring your résumé, but it should still be attended to with care.

Below is the cover letter I used to end my unemployment:

August 22, 2011

Dear Hiring Manager,

I am responding to your job posting for the position of Division Manager of Human Resources posted on the SHRM and City of Aurora websites. I recently left my position as the Director of Human Resources at one of the largest law firms in the western United States. Through my nearly twenty years of Human Resources experience, I have performed all of the tasks the position you list requires. Without going into exhaustive detail, following are a few of the specifics about my experience as they pertain to this position:

Legal compliance – I protected my firm from lawsuits by handling all disciplinary actions up to and including terminations using sound employment law practices. Despite working with a group (attorneys, paralegals and legal staff) that is much more litigiously minded than the non-legal population, over the course of ten years and 200+ terminations, there were no lawsuits filed against the firm for employment actions. In a recent performance review, one of the employment law partners with whom I work closely wrote: "Dan communicates very well; he knows when to talk and write like an employment lawyer, and when to talk and write like a Director of Human Resources."

Employee relations – over the years, frequent changes within my firm required effective employee relations and interpersonal skills. Mergers, acquisitions and recession-related changes in firm policy all required extensive ability to inspire and retain employees. As demonstration of success in this area, one retiring employee observed, "Dan put the human back in Human Resources."

Benefits design and administration – For the past decade, I have been responsible for benefits design and administration of our self-funded health benefits plan, as well as dental, vision, life, AD&D and long-term disability. I have redesigned our benefits offerings as necessary to limit cost increases while at the same time providing benefits that helped us attract and retain talent. In redesigning these benefits, I worked closely with our brokers as well as our ERISA and employment law attorneys to ensure compliance with all statutes and regulations. These efforts, along with strong negotiations, have saved our firm over $2,000,000 over the past five years.

Coaching and influencing – I was often called upon to coach department heads to ensure consistent and legal application of HR policies and procedures. This allowed us to deal with difficult situations in a smooth and professional manner, ensuring the firm was protected against adverse claims or lawsuits. In the ten years I was at the firm, not one lawsuit was filed against the firm for employment actions.

Employee development / training – for ten years I worked in a training division of a Fortune 20 company, exploring required competencies and developing and delivering training to close gaps in skills and performance. Most recently I developed, introduced and administered an internal training university, aimed at enhancing the skill set of our staff and providing job enrichment for them.

In addition to the 19 years Human Resources experience I bring to the table, I have an MBA, and I am SPHR certified.

I would be pleased to visit with you regarding this position to see how my skills and experience might help the City of Aurora exceed its strategic business initiatives and objectives. I can be reached at 303-555-1212 or wdanielquillen@gmail.com.

Thank you for your consideration,

Daniel Quillen

Note – even though this cover letter stretches over several pages in this book, it fits nicely onto one 8 1/2" x 11" page (written in Times New Roman and with 12-point font).

Let's discuss each of the sections of my cover letter:

DATE
"August 22, 2011"

As with all letters, you should date your cover letter. As I was tailoring my cover letters, this was one area I discovered I needed to be especially vigilant in: since I was using a template, I would occasionally forget to change the date at the top.

SALUTATION
"Dear Hiring Manager,"

Whether you use Dear Hiring Manager, Hiring Manager, Dear Recruiter, Human Resources Department or some other salutation, you should have some sort of salutation in your letter. The very best thing is if you can find the name of the actual hiring manager, and address the letter directly to her or him. We'll talk about ways to discover that person's name later. Avoid using salutations such as To Whom It May Concern and Dear Sir.

If you do have the name of the hiring manager, make certain you spell that name correctly. Also, is Chris Jones a man or a woman? Unless you know for certain, don't guess – if you're wrong it's bad. Consider using:

Dear Chris Jones,

If you know the hiring manager is a woman, do not use Miss or Mrs. in your salutation. Ms. is more than acceptable these days. If you are uncomfortable with that, then stay with Dear Cynthia Jones (and unless you know for sure, don't assume that Cynthia goes by Cindy).

Avoid addressing the hiring manager in a cover letter by their first name. While a generalization, this seems especially to be a tendency of Generation X and Y. Don't assume informality – a more formal greeting in your letter, as well as in person, is far more likely to impress than not. And besides, if you know the hiring manager's name is William, does he go by William, Will, Willie, Bill, Liam, or something else? Since I am one of many that goes by his middle name, I am always amused by people who assume informality with me and call me Bill (my first name is William). I suppose they are trying to establish a connection or rapport, but that's the wrong way to do that with me (and many others, I might add).

Don't be informal!

Should you use a comma or a colon? I prefer a comma, even though it is a business letter and a little more informal, but either will suffice. Do not confuse a colon (:) with a semi-colon (;) – they are not just different manifestations of the same punctuation mark. They have different uses, and if you are unsure which to use, find another punctuation mark!

OPENING PARAGRAPH
"I am responding to your job posting for the position of Division Manager of Human Resources posted on the SHRM and City of Aurora websites. I recently left my position as the Director of Human Resources at one of the largest law firms in the western United States. Through my nearly twenty

years of Human Resources experience, I have performed all of the tasks the position you list requires. Without going into exhaustive detail, following are a few of the specifics about my experience as they pertain to this position:"

This is a quick snapshot of who you are. As a hiring manager, I am always interested in which advertising or other source candidates found my job listing. This is especially important if you learned of this position through a friend or family member who works for that company – you want that information to be front and center.

Be sure and mention the title of the position for which you are applying, and if there is a job number associated with it, include that. For example:

> I am responding to the posting on the CareerBuilder website for a *Manager, Human Resources* (65796612) in Englewood, Colorado (reference ID 65805341_276281623).

Large companies in particular may have many positions listed simultaneously. If your cover letter says, "I am applying for the position I read about on your website," that's an invitation for your applications packet to find its way into the trash can. Busy HR departments and hiring managers don't have time to try and figure out which position you are interested in. Don't make it difficult on them.

Assuming your current position is relevant to the position you are seeking, tell them what your current or most recent position is / was. This begins to establish you as a credible candidate. If you are currently a sales manager, this helps identify you as a good candidate for my sales manager opening. If you are a barista or waitress, but are seeking a position as an interior designer, don't include your current position. Instead, open with something like: "I am seeking an opportunity to use my degree in interior design to further the success of Acme Interior Design Studios."

I tinkered a lot with the following sentences found at the end of the first paragraph:

> "Through my nearly twenty years of Human Resources experience, I have performed all of the tasks the position you list requires.

Without going into exhaustive detail, following are a few of the specifics about my experience as they pertain to this position:"

Earlier I informed the hiring manager that I was a Human Resources professional. This sentence expands that by sharing my years of experience. Then I prepare them for the next section of my letter – I tell them I have experience in all the areas they are seeking (only say that if it's true…you will have to modify this if not), and am going to share my experience *as it relates to the position they posted*. Just as in your résumé, you want to highlight the aspects of your current job and career that specifically address those things identified in the job ad as being important to the hiring manager.

Remember during the *Résumés* chapter we talked about the need to print out the job description and circle the key elements of the job? You used that exercise to identify the nine bullet points that would go in your *Summary of Qualifications* section. Those same elements are important for your cover letter also. Except in your cover letter, you probably won't have the space to do more than four of five of them, so pick the four or five you feel are the most crucial for this position.

You might ask if it's okay to use the same elements in both your résumé as well as your cover letter. My answer is "Yes!" Remember – we mentioned some hiring managers only read cover letters and others only read résumés. Some read both. Let's not overlook members of the hiring manager population who may only read one or the other document.

In my résumé, each of the skills and experience areas has associated accomplishments listed. This is important in your cover letter and in your résumé.

Remember – you are trying to convince some faceless person on the other end of the job search line that you have what it takes to help their company succeed. What better way than to outline the skills and experiences they are seeking and show how you have excelled in each of those areas?

MINIMUM QUALIFICATIONS
"In addition to the 19 years Human Resources experience I bring to the table, I have an MBA, and I am SPHR certified."

Most positions today have a *Minimum Qualifications* section in their job ad clearly outlining the company's expectations regarding education, experience, licenses, certifications, etc. This sentence allows you to address how you stack up against those requirements. If you don't meet their minimum requirements in one (or more) of the areas, I wouldn't highlight it here.

Often, you'll see *Minimum Requirements* listed with a certain level of education (typically Bachelors degree required, Masters degree preferred), or relevant work experience. That last little tag line allows the company some wiggle room to hire someone without a degree, and often cracks the door open a bit for candidates who have tremendous experience but no formal degree.

CLOSING PARAGRAPH
"I would be pleased to visit with you regarding this position to see how my skills and experience might help the City of Aurora exceed its strategic business initiatives and objectives. I can be reached at 303-555-1212 or wdanielquillen@gmail.com."

Remember, when you are applying for a job, it's not all about YOU, but all about what the hiring manager wants and needs. You just need to convince the manager that *you* are who they need to solve their problems.

In the past I have received advice that you should put a date that you'll be following up: "I'll call you next Tuesday to follow up on my résumé to see if you have any questions." I am not a big fan of that. In fact, it's a little off-putting to me. It seems too forward and aggressive.

Don't forget to always list your contact number and your e-mail address.

CLOSING
"Thank you for your consideration,"

I think anything here that is respectful is fine. *Respectfully, Regards, Sincerely* or the like are all fine.

Once again, I would avoid being too informal: Don't close with "Thanks!" I even prefer *Thank you for your consideration* over *Thanks for your consideration.* I don't think it is a big deal, but I do prefer the former.

COVER LETTER TEMPLATE

You may recall from the *Résumés* chapter one of the tools I use is a résumé template to tailor my résumé and make that process more streamlined. This template has all the key components of my résumé, along with thirty-five bullet points of my experiences and accomplishments. By taking the time to write each of these and place them in a template, they are available to cut and paste and insert into my tailored résumé, already having been scrubbed for content, grammar, typos, and accomplishments.

Likewise, I developed a cover letter template, filled with insertions that can be used to tailor my cover letter for any position for which I am applying. While my cover letter is one page, my cover letter *template* is six pages. And while the average cover letter may have four or five job experiences listed, my template has over fifty items. Each of these items was written in response to a job ad that called for expertise in one of these areas. Following are the first few entries in my cover letter template:

Article writing – during my time with AT&T corporate marketing, I was co-editor of a newsletter that was sent to over 20,000 of our key clients each month. I frequently wrote articles for the newsletter. While Director of Human Resources with my current firm, I also wrote several articles for publication: one for the national SHRM website as well as an article for *The Colorado Lawyer*. I am also a freelance author, having written fourteen published books and numerous articles in national publications.

Benefits design and administration – For the past decade, I have been responsible for benefits design and administration of our self-funded health benefits plan, as well as dental, vision, life, AD&D and long-term disability. I have redesigned our benefits offerings as necessary to limit cost increases while at the same time providing benefits that helped us attract and retain talent. In redesigning these benefits, I have worked closely with our brokers as well as our ERISA and employment law attorneys to ensure compliance with all statutes and regulations. These efforts, along with strong negotiations, have saved our firm over $2,000,000 over the past five years.

Best-in-class Human Resources – I was fortunate to learn the HR craft at a Fortune 20 company (AT&T), which had the resources and vision to ensure their HR practices were best-in-class. I brought this best-in-class mentality and practices to the law firm where I worked as Director of Human Resources for the past ten years.

Broad knowledge of Human Resources – through my nearly two decades of HR practice, I have developed a broad platform of HR knowledge and experience, including strategic planning, organizational development, recruiting, talent management and development, succession planning, benefits selection and administration, etc. These skills have allowed me to support my organizations across a broad spectrum of areas, enabling them to be as efficient and profitable as possible.

Note that each entry begins with the category of the entry: *Article writing, Benefits design and administration, Best-in-class Human Resources*, etc. I have these listed alphabetically in my cover letter template for ease of location, but in my cover letter, I lead with the elements that seem most critical to the hiring manager of the position for which I am applying (that is – they are *not* listed alphabetically in my cover letter).

Many of my entries are duplicates of others, except for the title / category of the entry. You may recall in the *Résumés* chapter I strongly encouraged you to use the hiring company's language. If they called it *Recruiting*, you should use the term *Recruiting* in your cover letter. If they use *Talent Acquisition*, then that's the term you should use.

E-MAIL VS ATTACHMENT

I have had discussions with a number of Directors of HR and other hiring managers about whether they like cover letters to be attachments to an e-mail, or whether they prefer them to be embedded in the e-mail itself. I spoke with many such managers, and the resounding answer was: "It doesn't matter."

The fact of the matter is, however, that depending on the industry, most cover letters and résumés will end up as attachments or cut-and-paste posts in application software. More on that in the *Gatekeepers* chapter.

If you decide to include your résumé as an attachment, you should provide it in pdf format. Otherwise, all that formatting you went to such great pains to work through may get lost when opened by the hiring manager.

SUMMARY

Here's the bottom line on cover letters:

- use them;
- make certain they are professional;
- no typos or grammar difficulties;
- highlight your skills as they relate to the job;
- include accomplishments;
- not too informal.

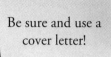

Be sure and use a
cover letter!

8. STAY POSITIVE

A strong, positive self-image is the best possible preparation for success.
– Joyce Brothers

When I was first laid off, I attended a job search session offered by my church. One of the things that struck me was a discussion we had about the wide-ranging emotions associated with having lost a job, including relief, shock, denial, self-isolation, anger, remorse, guilt, panic, depression, resignation, acceptance, building, optimism and elation.

The leaders of the workshop I attended hastened to point out that these emotions weren't necessarily sequential, and you might leap ahead (to optimism and elation when you get an interview) or fall back (to resignation or panic when you hear you didn't get the job).

I have several friends who have been unemployed for long periods of time – years. Based on my working with them, I'd say each of them has experienced these emotions at one time or another in their job hunt.

I am by nature a very optimistic person, so I didn't experience some of the more difficult emotions listed here – depression and panic. But I did find myself needing to fight many of the more negative emotions.

So – be prepared for a wide range of feelings, and map a strategy to deal with the difficult situation you are facing.

You have already started doing that through the pages of this book. You are taking the first steps to placing yourself in the Land of the Employed once again: you're learning how to attack this challenge that has come your way. I think one of the most valuable tools in your job hunt will be the ability to remain positive. Hundreds of books and articles have been written on the power of positive thinking, and you need to believe every one of them!

I have developed ten keys to staying positive during this trying time in your life. Let's see if you agree with them:

KEY #1 – KEEP BUSY

One of the best things you can do to ward off depression is to keep busy. Prepare for battle, launch your résumés and cover letters into the great unknown at an unprecedented pace. Don't fire without targets, and don't fire ill-prepared ammunition. You need to plan your attack, prepare your weapons (your résumé and cover letter), and identify companies for whom you are qualified to work. Plan how you will get résumé screeners to put yours in the *Call-for-an-Interview* pile.

KEY #2 – START AN EXERCISE PROGRAM

Exercise is a great tool to battle depression. Select a time during the day that you will exercise, and stick to that schedule. Some people are morning people, and early mornings are a great time to exercise. However – you have to know yourself well. I know, for example, that any exercise program I start in the early morning hours is doomed to failure. I am one of those people that, if I was the one making the rules, early morning meetings would be held at 10:00am or 10:30am in the morning. Five o'clock only occurs once a day on my clock, and it is usually followed shortly thereafter by sunset.

I'd suggest exercising at least five, if not six days per week. I am a big believer in Sunday being a day of rest, and that makes sense for my exercising muscles too. The exercise I chose was to walk daily, Monday through Saturday.

KEY #3 – CHANGE YOUR MINDSET

Surprisingly, this was one of the more difficult aspects of the job search for me. Prior to my lay-off, we were pretty comfortable financially. We could buy things more or less at whim (within reason, of course. We couldn't, for example, buy the Dodgers when they were for sale…). I am a book fiend, and buy many books each year. Twenty minutes on Amazon.com and I could easily drop $200 or more, and this sometimes happened several times each month. I found I could no longer do that – I needed to shepherd my resources. I became a coupon clipper for the first time in my life.

This was a hard adjustment to make. Frankly, it was probably a good adjustment to make, as on a monthly basis, we were seeing hundreds of dollars slip out of our budget for non-essential items. Once I finally got my mindset changed, it was easy to do. But the first little while it was difficult.

KEY #4 — MARSHAL YOUR RESOURCES

Immediately upon your change of employment status, determine what resources are available to you. What cash reserves do you have? If you needed to cash in a portion of (or borrow from) your 401(k), could you? What revenues are coming in and what expenses demand payment? In a severe pinch, could a family member help out?

Are there expenses you can do without? Our home phone, internet and cable TV bill is close to $200 per month. We have cell phones, so we could certainly do without the cable TV and our home phone. That would save us a chunk of change. (We'd still need our Internet for job searching.) Do you have similar expenses? Are there corners you can cut? I have a friend who lost his job in May, and immediately sold his ski boat. He figured if he waited until the end of the water skiing season, he might be unable to sell the boat, or if he was able to sell it, he'd have to take less money for it. He traded in his wife's BMW for a car that was still functional but much less expensive. He economized.

You may want to look for something part-time to do to make ends meet. If you do that, be careful not to accept so many hours that you cannot conduct an effective job search. I've a friend who worked part-time for a moving company during his period of unemployment, and that allowed him the flexibility to work around the times he had set for his job search.

You have children in college with large tuition payments due? Rather than pay those tuition expenses out of your savings, consider getting student loans. Even if you don't want your children saddled with those debts once they get out of college, you can still do that. Just do this with the understanding that you will make the loan payments when the time comes.

We stopped going out to eat. Whereas we were going out to eat once or twice a week, we curtailed that expense and saved plenty.

One of the first things I did was figure out the maze of requirements to apply for unemployment benefits, and did so. As mentioned earlier in the book, it often takes six weeks or so for unemployment benefits to kick in.

KEY #5 – REMEMBER, 20,000,000+ AMERICANS

If you are unemployed in America, as of this writing, you share that stage with 20,000,000+ Americans. The government only considers about half that number as unemployed…the others they assume have given up job hunting, so they don't include them in the official unemployment figures. I suspect that may be correct for some, but truly believe most of that 20,000,000+ should be counted as unemployed. Regardless – a LOT of people are out of work right now, many of them through no fault of their own. Good people are hitting the streets. Unfortunately, you are one of those good people.

While the saying goes, *Misery loves company*, that's not my point. My point is that you are not alone. You have not been singled out as the only one to lose his or her job. Keep the proper perspective: you and millions of other outstanding people – top performers, bright (even brilliant) people, innovators, hard workers, etc., have lost their job. Okay, that's a fact. But don't dwell on your loss so much that you miss opportunities that may be open to you.

KEY #6 – DON'T BE A VICTIM

I think this is an important consideration. What happened, happened. Don't waste your time blaming others, wondering how on earth management could have made that decision to let you go, etc. Sometimes that negative thinking comes through in your cover letters, and often even in your job interviews. You cannot afford for that to happen.

Remember – I am not alone!

Near the end of my job search, it came to light that some companies in the United States were advertising that the unemployed need not apply, that they were only seeking currently employed applicants. I figure this must have seemed like a good idea to someone (probably someone who had never been unemployed – who may well be soon!), but they didn't pause to consider the public relations nightmare it would cause for their company. What a short-sighted, mean-spirited approach to hiring.

Don't let those comments bother you. There will always be mean-spirited people like that in every walk of life, and I suppose VPs of Human Resources are no different – some can be like that. Who cares? To be honest, I wouldn't want to work for a company that treated people like that anyway!

As a hiring manager, I understood clearly that with the ups and downs of the economy in recent years, there was a great deal of outstanding talent on the outside looking in. Of course I needed to do my due diligence when interviewing someone who had been laid off: asking them why they were let go, checking references, etc. But if I liked you as a candidate and you weren't currently employed, it was a bonus for me: that meant you could start the next day, and I wouldn't have to wait for you to give two-weeks' notice, then run the risk of your current company countering my offer, etc. It is a win-win situation for all of us!

KEY #7 – SET A SCHEDULE
Earlier in this book, I spent quite a bit of time speaking about setting a schedule and sticking to it. I reiterate that counsel here. If you are busy doing something productive with your time, the time will pass quickly, you won't sit around and brood or worry about your unemployed status, etc. Your job now is to find a job, and you should set a schedule and stick to it.

KEY #8 – GET PLENTY OF SLEEP
Getting plenty of sleep is important, as it will help you deal with the depression and self-defeating doubts that might creep in occasionally. One of the best bits of advice I received at the time of my lay-off was to get good, consistent sleep. Occasionally I stayed up way later than normal, but generally speaking, I was in bed most nights by 10:00pm and arose most mornings by 7:00am.

KEY #9 – PREPARE FOR THE LONG HAUL
At the time of this writing, our economy is improving somewhat. But it is so fragile. An unexpected jobs report, a lower earnings (or loss) report of a Fortune 200 company, unrest in the Middle East, and a host of other such

calamities (or risks of calamity) can cause the economy to reel and step back a few paces.

Experts reportedly claim that it takes a month of job searching for every $10,000 of income you are trying to replace. So, if you're trying to find a $70,000 job, plan on being out of work seven months. The first time I heard this, the economy was strong, so it may even take more time to find a job in this New Economy.

Set your expectations appropriately, or you risk being disappointed. If you feel you'll be employed in two weeks, then I am afraid you may be disappointed. The key is to work as though you will be able to be employed in two weeks if you work hard, but be realistic in the expectation that it may take longer than that to find a new job.

Statistics show the average worker who is laid off can expect a 25% to 40% cut in pay when s/he does go back to work. In my case, I took a 33% cut in pay when I returned to work, so I'd have to say that statement is pretty accurate – I am a pretty average guy. I have known a few who actually increased their pay, but mostly my friends and acquaintances have reported a loss of earnings when returning to work.

KEY #10 – BUILD IN SOME ENTERTAINMENT

All work and no play makes Jack (and Jill) a dull boy (and girl). Make some time for yourself. Make time for your family – remember, everyone who loves you and in particular those who live under the same roof is sharing this experience with you, in one way or another.

When I told my mother I had been laid off, she said, referring to our two oldest children: "Oh, this would be a great time for you to go visit Katie in Chicago and Michael in Portland." I said yes, if it weren't for the need to be cautious with our money at this time. Of course it would be unwise to take that round-the-world trip you've always wanted to take, or pack up the kids and head for Disney World.

But, depending on where you live, a drive in the mountains or a trip to the nearby ocean to see the sunset are inexpensive ways to spend time together and get out of the house. Perhaps a trip to the mall as a family, looking for the most outrageous window display you can find would keep everyone's spirits up. Or just a picnic in the park. We like Redbox movies – even on a tightened-belt budget we feel we can afford to rent a movie or two at Redbox.

How about learning to play that musical instrument you've always wanted to take up? Begin teaching yourself a foreign language. Brush up on old skills, learn new ones in your field ... the list goes on and on!

Whatever it takes, don't allow yourself to slip into the doldrums.

KEY #11 – HANG IN THERE!

Finally, hang in there. This time in your life will be over sooner than you think. Hopefully in the future as you look back on this experience, you can do so with introspection and insight, perhaps even fondness. It is easy to be professional when everything is going your way. But real professionalism manifests itself during adversity.

(You'll note I said I had ten keys, but provided eleven. Well, I am a firm believer in not over-committing, and in always providing more than promised....)

9. GATEKEEPERS

Obstacles don't have to stop you. If you run into a wall, don't turn around and give up. Figure out how to climb it, go through it, or work around it.
— Michael Jordan

During your job search, you will encounter gatekeepers – those who will do their best to keep you away from your intended target – the hiring manager — and your ultimate target – a new job. In this chapter we'll discuss several of them, and how to overcome their best efforts to screen you out.

APPLICATIONS SOFTWARE
During your job search, you'll almost assuredly run into *applications software*. These sophisticated tools of Human Resource departments provide the first hoop for you to jump through. Refusing to do so, or trying to game the system, will result in no interview and no job, regardless of how qualified you are.

If you have not searched for a job in recent years, this may be a new experience for you. But it is one you'll likely not be able to avoid. During my recent job search, I submitted my application for 130 jobs. Of those jobs, approximately 115 of them funneled all applicants through applications software.

And what does this applications software do? At its basic level, it provides screening assistance for busy HR departments and hiring managers: it screens *in* some applicants, and screens *out* others. Let me provide several examples:

Let's say a company has advertised a job with the following minimum requirements:

Must have a Bachelors degree, Master's degree preferred. Must have PHR, SPHR and / or CEBS certification.

Successful applicants will have a minimum of six years of experience in this field.

Must have complete fluency in Spanish, including reading, writing and speaking.

The company's applications software will be programmed to ask a series of job-relevant questions. Samples of possible questions include:

1.How many years experience do you have in XYZ field?
a. 0 to 2
b. 3 to 5
c. 6 to 10
d. more than 10

2. Do you have a Bachelors degree?
a. Yes
b. No

3. Do you have a Masters degree?
a. Yes
b. No

4. This position requires fluency in Spanish. At what level are you fluent?
a. Reading, writing and speaking.
b. Reading only.
c. Speaking only.
d. Writing only.

5. Do you have current PHR, SPHR or CEBS certification?
a. Yes
b. No

All rather benign questions, wouldn't you agree? But an HR department or hiring manager can instruct the applications software to screen out those applicants whose answers indicate they don't meet the minimum requirements of the job. Your application may go no further than this faceless, nameless – and very effective – gatekeeper.

More sophisticated applications software also scan an applicant's résumé for skills and experiences that are important to the hiring manager and required for the job. Like the example above, it can review your résumé in microseconds and accept – or reject — it based on whether it finds certain key words and phrases. You could be the most qualified candidate for the position, but if your résumé doesn't possess the correct words and phrases, it will be rejected, and your résumé will never even make it to the hiring manager for her or his review. That's why in the *Résumés* chapter, I stressed using the company's words from the job description in your résumé.

Don't believe me? Let me give you a very concrete example that happened to me.

Early in my job hunt, I found myself up late one night / early one morning. I was searching for work when I ran across a position that looked interesting, and began tailoring my résumé. I printed off the job description, circled the critical elements, then began tailoring away. While I had experience in most of the areas the job required, there were a few areas of experience I was short on. I decided to submit anyway. After readying my résumé, I went to the applications software and uploaded it. It was 2:46am.

Immediately I received an e-mail from the company, acknowledging my submission. Here is the e-mail (I added the **bolding,** and redacted the company's name):

> From: _____ Company donotreply@trm.brassring.com
> To: wdanielquillen@gmail.com
> Date: **Mon, Jul 18, 2011 at 2:46 AM**
> Subject: Your candidate reference number - _____ Company.
>
> Thank you, W Quillen, for expressing interest in _____.
>
> We have successfully received your submission to the following position(s):

Training and Development Coordinator 18730BR

Your background, skills and experience will be reviewed against the position you have selected. Your résumé will also remain on file for your use when exploring future _____ career opportunities.

As a world leader in defense electronics, _____ Company is committed to providing challenging and rewarding opportunities.

Please continue to investigate other positions with _____ and submit your résumé to those that are of interest.

Sincerely,
_____ Talent Acquisition Team

Ten minutes later, I received the following e-mail at 2:56am:

From:AutomationManager@brassring.com,
Enterprise@trm.brassring.com
To: wdanielquillen@gmail.com
Date: **Mon, Jul 18, 2011 at 2:56 AM**
Subject: Regarding Your _____ Job Submission

Dear W,

Thank you for submitting your résumé for the position of Training and Development Coordinator, Req ID 18730BR.

Your background and qualifications have been given careful review with respect to this position. Although you were not selected for this position, we appreciate your desire to expand your career. Please check your Job Submission status to get the most updated status of other _____ opportunities to which you have applied.

Please continue to investigate other job postings with _____ and apply to any that are commensurate with your background and experience. Again, thank you for your interest in _____.

Sincerely,

_____ Talent Acquisition Team

Note the statement in the second paragraph:

Your background and qualifications have been given careful review with respect to this position. Although you were not selected for this position, we appreciate your desire to expand your career.

Forgive my skepticism, but I seriously doubt there was a recruiter / member of the HR team sitting at their desk at 2:46am on July 18, 2011, just waiting for résumés to pop into their e-mail inbox so they could *carefully* review them. (It is true that many members of HR departments are over-worked, but I suspect that's not what was happening here.) The "careful review" of my background and qualifications was in all likelihood performed by applications software – in this case Brass Ring, one of the leading application software systems in the industry.

But don't dismay. If you follow the suggestions I have made throughout this book, it will increase your chances of getting past this initial gatekeeper. Another important thing to keep in mind is this: follow the instructions. Just like the need to be obedient in elementary school:

• raise your hand before you speak;
• walk — don't run;
• no cutting in line;
• put your name on your paper;
• etc.

You must follow the instructions presented to you in the applications software. Several critical instructions I have seen include:

1. Complete and thorough responses to the following questions are necessary in order to be considered for this vacancy and move to the next step in the recruitment process.

2. Please provide a detailed description of your job responsibilities for each position. Do not type, "See Résumé."

In various forms, I ran across item *Number 1* above in numerous applications front-ends during my job search, the last of which was with the entity at which I was hired – the City of Aurora, Colorado. It is a standard instruction we put at the beginning of most applications. After reviewing hundreds of applications for the city, it is amazing to me how many candidates ignore that instruction, and it almost always seems to mean that they also ignore *Number 2* above. And I'll tell you how the recruiters in my department handle those applications: they reject them with the notation: "Did not follow application instructions."

Okay, so you're a maverick and like to blaze your own trail. I get that. But don't do it during the application process.

Fill out all applications completely!

HUMAN RESOURCES DEPARTMENTS

HR departments also serve as gatekeepers through whom you (or your résumé) must pass to get to the hiring managers. In many companies, HR organizations screen résumés for hiring managers, handing off to them the top three to six résumés that come in. Each department does it a little differently – some do it manually, some use applications software to do the first screen, then they do the next level of screening.

At this stage of the process, think of HR departments as human applications software: they screen resumes, searching for those that meet the minimum requirements of the position – education, experience, certifications, etc., often culling the stack of resumes first using those criteria. Once they have a more manageable pile of resumes to review, then they review looking for specific experience, accomplishments – things that say, "This candidate is Top Notch," etc.

EXECUTIVE ASSISTANTS

Executive assistants can provide a formidable hurdle to get around as you try to gain access to the hiring manager. They are good at protecting their manager from intrusions throughout the day, and in many cases, s/he will lump you into the *Intrusions* category.

Executive assistants come into play, of course, only if you have gotten to the hiring manager level of the hiring process. This can happen in several ways:

- you are aware of who the hiring manager is through your network of friends and professional colleagues;
- you have found the hiring manager's name by calling the company, checking out their website, or even from the job ad itself;
- the hiring manager has posted a position on Facebook, Twitter, LinkedIn, etc.
- You have interviewed with, or been contacted by, the hiring manager for the position in question;
- any creative way you can find him / her.

Regardless of how you are in possession of the hiring manager's name, the executive assistant stands ready to stymie your efforts to get through to your potential manager. And they are often very good at what they do.

And, before I give you the tip that will help you get past this Gatekeeper, let me tell you that executive assistants are far more powerful and influential than many people realize. Often, hiring managers will ask their executive assistant what they think about a candidate. If you have been short with him or her, rude, frustrated, etc., you can bet this assistant will share that insight – and it *will* be listened to. First of all, I understand you should be polite and professional to everyone you meet. But it is imperative that you are on your very best behavior (as my mother would say) in all your dealings with the hiring manager's executive assistant.

That isn't to say you shouldn't try to get around their gatekeeping efforts. Here is the key: while most executive assistants work hard, they often work 8:00am to 5:00pm, while their managers may be working 7:30am to 6:00pm or later. So here's the hint – call before formal business hours or call after the workday has ended. Call during the lunch hour. While the executive assistant may be off during those times, the hiring manager often is not. If you try at 7:30am and the executive assistant answers, then try after hours – 5:30pm, for example.

We'll talk later about reasons you may be calling the hiring manager, but for now, expect your calls to be intercepted efficiently, politely and professionally by the executive assistant.

10. BEFORE THE INTERVIEW

One important key to success is self-confidence. An important key to self-confidence is preparation. – Arthur Ashe

I have spent many hours in locker rooms before athletic contests. Taped ankles and wrists, stretching, icing, the guy in the corner by himself, concentrating on shutting out all the hub-bub and trying to mentally prepare for the upcoming contest. All are part of the pre-game preparation.

Before arriving in the locker room prior to the Big Game, more preparation occurred – drills on the most basic elements of the game – tackling drills, wind sprints, agility drills, running the bases, taking batting practice, "turning two," swimming laps, kick turns, practicing takedowns, reverses and holds.

All in preparation for the Big Game.

And that's what you need to be about prior to *your* Big Game – The Interview.

Congratulations – you made the cut – not only are you on the varsity team, you're starting the game. You know you need to prove yourself. The spotlight is on you.

Time to review your preparation, to psych yourself up to peak performance.

NETWORKS
Earlier in Chapter 3, we talked about identifying a network of individuals who could help you in your job search. Now that you've gotten an interview, use your network again.

Send a short note to your network, something along the lines of:

> All,
>
> Thanks for your work on my behalf these past few months. I have good news — later this week I have an interview with Acme Company. The hiring manager with whom I will be meeting is Robert Smith.
>
> I would love to hear from anyone who knows Mr. Smith, Acme or anyone who works at Acme. Any insights, thoughts and / or putting in a good word on my behalf would be appreciated.
>
> Regards,
>
> Dan

RESEARCH

An important part of your job search comes when you have been contacted to come in for an interview. Immediately you should begin learning all you can about the company with which you will be interviewing.

Become extremely familiar with all aspects of this company. Go to their website and follow every link, read every scrap of information you can find, so that you learn all you can about the company. Read newspaper stories (easily obtained on the Internet), comments on investment websites, etc.

One of my favorite sources of information on companies is their *Annual Report*. All publically traded companies have annual reports, and most can be found online. These reports can be a gold mine of company information. They almost always have an introduction from the CEO or president of the company. They will often provide information about company strategies (e.g., expanding their European markets, focusing on the Pacific Northwest, etc.). Comments about recent mergers – or proposed mergers, recent acquisitions, divestitures, etc., are all good information to have in your back pocket as you head into your interview.

I have preached this principle many times in recent years to those with whom I have met to assist in their job searches, and I almost always follow that counsel myself. And yet, notwithstanding that, I went to a job interview after having scanned the company's website in a perfunctory manner. May I tell you my chagrin when the first question I was asked in the interview was: "What do you know about our company?" Here was an opportunity to shine by showing how informed I was about their company history, current markets, growth and strategy, etc. I failed miserably. My mind nearly went blank – because there was precious little in there about this company. I uttered a few thoughts, but even to me it sounded pretty lame. I kicked myself for the rest of the interview, and I daresay it negatively affected my performance during the rest of the time with the hiring manager. It was, to put it bluntly, an opportunity missed.

And I knew better! So don't find yourself in the same situation – prepare! If you aren't asked, "What do you know about our company?" during the interview, you should find a way to work your knowledge in. For example, at the end of most interviews I have been on, I have been asked, "Do you have any questions for me?" This is your opportunity to show them you have an interest in the company beyond merely interviewing for a job. "Why yes, I do. In your most recent annual report I see where your CEO, Mr. Brown, said you were 'going full-speed ahead' into Europe. Will that move have any impact on the department I will be working in?"

> Research the
> companies I
> interview with!

DRESS FOR SUCCESS

I have always been a proponent of dressing well for job interviews. By "dressing well," I mean dressing a notch or two above the norm for the office.

Let's briefly discuss each element of your dress:

Suit

Classic-cut suits are the best. First of all, you don't have to replace your suit every time fashions change. Dark suits are my preference – blue, blue pinstripe or gray – very conservative. I am not a fan of black because they feel…funeral-ish.

In the 1980s, it was fashionable for women to wear a white shirt, dark blue skirt and jacket, accentuated with a feminine red tie – the power colors. That is no longer necessary. Women no longer have to look like men when interviewing for a position. They do, however, need to dress professionally. As with men, dark colors are important, although women can get away with warmer colors like brown or green.

Shirt
I recommend either a white shirt or a very light blue shirt, but white is preferable.

Your shirt and suit should be recently cleaned and pressed. When I first started my job hunt, my job coach gave me some of the best advice I received during my search: he told me to reserve my "interview suit," shirt and tie just for that purpose. Both your suit and shirt should be freshly cleaned. Your shirt should be starched – it only costs about $1.50 – after each wearing. I prefer heavy starch, but medium or light would do. I recall feeling like a million bucks when I "suited up" for an interview wearing my suit pants with the crisp crease and my gleaming starched white shirt.

Women's blouses should be conservative and certainly not provocative. Sheer, tight-fitting blouses have no place in the business world and especially not at a job interview. Nylons are essential for your job interview.

Interviewers appreciate both men and women who come to job interviews dressed conservatively and professionally.

Tie
Add to your interview suit a conservative – not too skinny and not too wide – red or blue tie. It, too, should be freshly pressed, but you don't need to dry clean it after every interview unless it has gotten wrinkled or had something spilled on it. A serviceable tie can be purchased for under $25. (Need I say no ties with cartoon characters, holiday messages, political statements or beer product advertising should be worn?)

Belt
Don't forget a conservative business belt. Like your tie, it should be of conservative width (not too thin and not too wide), with a simple silver or gold clasp. It should match the color of your shoes, which should be black. You can pick up such a belt for $15 to $20 at Wal-Mart, Kohl's, Pennys, Sears, etc.

For women, if your outfit needs or takes a belt, by all means accessorize. But the same rule applies to women as it does to men – belts should be conservative and not flashy or extreme.

Shoes

Okay, your shoes don't have to be wingtips, but black, conservative shoes should be your goal. Perhaps you have seen the television clip from a number of years ago when comedian George Gobel was on the *Johnny Carson Show*. He quipped, "Did you ever get the feeling the world was a tuxedo and you were a pair of brown shoes?" Notwithstanding the fact his comment was made several decades ago, the point is still a valid one: dark suits and brown shoes don't go together. So be aware and conscious of that when you dress for success.

Your shoes should be freshly polished to a high gleam.

Women should also wear conservative shoes. A pump or moderate heel is fine, but you shouldn't wear spike heels to your job interview. And ladies – don't forget to polish your shoes also. If you are short, you might consider a little higher heel; conversely, if you are already tall, you might go with lower heels or flats.

Are my shoes shined?

Socks

By now you've probably figured out that I recommend conservative socks with your suit. Now is not the time to make a statement. Even if it's Christmas time, please don't wear socks with reindeer and Santa on them.

Women should always wear nylons to job interviews.

Jewelry

The rule of thumb for successful interviewing is to go easy on the jewelry. If you have a heavy bracelet or watch that clunks on the table whenever you write, it would be best to leave that particular item of jewelry home. Women – your earrings and necklaces should not be flashy – dangling earrings or heavy necklaces may draw attention away from the real message you are trying to get across.

Piercings – beyond earrings – are another matter you'll have to decide for yourself, I am afraid. Piercings are much more acceptable today than they were just a few years ago. However, many employers with customer-facing openings (sales, receptionists, etc.) are hesitant to hire those with significant piercings.

Okay – I know there are a number of you out there saying, "Whoa – if I wore a suit to my job interview at a construction company (heavy equipment company, trucking company, etc.) they would laugh me out of the building. That may be true – actually probably would be true. In those cases I would dress several levels above what you expect to see in the office. Blue jeans and t-shirts are the accepted office apparel? Then I would opt to wear a pair of clean and well-pressed khakis and a collared shirt. If business casual is the dress code (khakis and collared shirts), I suggest you wear a pair of slacks, a white or light blue shirt, and a tie. Perhaps even a sports coat.

I once managed a training center, where my instructors taught classes to individuals who installed large telephone systems, computers, etc. The students were classic blue-collar workers, many of whom were pretty rough around the edges. Dress code for my instructors was business casual; most wore khakis, collared shirts and ties – their choice – but some didn't wear ties.

Occasionally I had to replace an instructor who had retired or moved on. The ideal candidate for the instructor position came from the ranks of our installers, because the technical ability and having "been there in the trenches" were critical to their knowledge, credibility, and success. When I interviewed candidates, their dress ranged from dirty blue jeans to suits and ties. I have to admit, my impressions were formed quickly, notwithstanding I knew the ideal candidate's dress was less important than his technical skills and experience. If I recall correctly, through the years, I didn't hire any of the candidates who showed up in dirty blue jeans. I'd guess my hiring was pretty evenly divided between the candidates who wore suits and those who wore business casual clothing.

Having said that, let me share a story my job coach told me. He was working with a Public Relations executive. The PR guy had several interviews with a dot.com-type software company for a six-figure position. Finally the call he was hoping for came: the CEO wanted to have lunch with him at an upscale restaurant. He was excited for the opportunity and knew he was on the threshold of ending his unemployment and going to work for a premier company.

Because he felt the work environment at the company was pretty casual, he had worn slacks, a sports coat and tie to both of his previous interviews. None of the managers with whom he interviewed wore ties – they were dressed in khakis and collared shirts. He had decided to dress like the company's managers for his meeting with the CEO – business casual. But he was uncertain enough about his decision that he called his job coach to get his input. His job coach strongly recommended the candidate wear his interview suit. They discussed and debated the issue at length, but the more his job coach recommended a suit, the more firm the candidate became in his position of dressing more casually. He did agree to wear a tie, which he felt was a huge concession.

The day of the lunch interview finally came. The candidate got to the restaurant early and waited excitedly for the CEO to arrive. Imagine his shock – and discomfort – when the CEO walked through the restaurant doors wearing an expensive suit, gleaming white shirt and conservative red tie! When they shook hands, the candidate noticed expensive gold cuff links on the CEO's monogrammed shirt sleeves. They exchanged small talk on the way to their table. Once settled, the following conversation ensued:

> CEO: "I reviewed your résumé and was very impressed with your education and experience. My managers spoke highly of your professionalism and capabilities. I know how PR executives are always concerned with appearances, so I wanted to show you how much I respected you as a candidate by wearing my best suit for our meeting today."

> The candidate knew he was toast. Thinking quickly, he said, "Well, thank you – you are most kind to say that. I know your company has a business casual dress code, so I dressed this way so I wouldn't make you feel uncomfortable. It seems we out-guessed one another!"

Nice try. The PR candidate didn't get the job, most likely because he made the wrong wardrobe decision.

Personally, I would prefer to risk being a little overdressed to being dressed too casually for an interview.

QUESTIONS

If you do nothing else I recommend in this chapter, you should pay particular attention to this next section and follow it to the letter. I will say that again, just to add emphasis:

> *If you do nothing else I recommend in this chapter, you should pay particular attention to this next section and follow it to the letter.*

Before your interview, you should try to come up with as many questions as you think may be asked during the interview. Focus first on the job description and requirements you read in the job ad. How do you stack up against the requirements for the position? What questions might be asked of you as they relate to the position? If you were the hiring manager, what questions would you ask a candidate for this position?

Once you have identified your list of questions, *write them down*. And then – and this is important – once you have written down the questions, *write down the answers!* This is the time to do that – when there is no pressure on you. Think each question through, think about the best answer possible, and write it down. Don't just *think* it out, but *write* it out. This gives you the opportunity to work out sentences and present your answer in the most powerful way possible.

Be honest in your answers. Also – look for ways you can answer the question that will make your hiring manager realize that you would bring a lot of value to their company if they hire you.

The questions you write down and then answer should fall into two categories:

1. Generic questions about your background and experience, and
2. Questions specific to the job itself.

Following are some of the generic questions I wrote down. I had a rather lengthy list of these questions (about 30) I reviewed before each job interview. Initially it took me quite a bit of time to come up with the answers, but since I wrote them down, they became a "study guide" for me before each interview. It was easy to run down the list of questions and refresh my memory.

Generic Questions

Question: Tell me about a time when you had a difficult situation with a co-worker.

Answer: A few years ago we got a new director of legal recruiting at my firm. Andrea was a hard driving, get-it-done-at-any-cost leader. She was a tremendous recruiter, finding exceptional talent for our organization. However, sometimes, in her zeal to bring the best talent into the firm, she made offers that caused problems for the existing workforce (or more particularly, for management!). For example, at our firm, we awarded the title of Senior Associate to those attorneys who had at least five years legal experience, two of which had to be at our law firm.

To get top talent, Andrea would sometimes extend offers to experienced attorneys with the promise that they would come into the firm as a Senior Associate. Since these candidates didn't have two years experience with our firm, bringing them in as Senior Associates was unfair to experienced attorneys already at our firm who were waiting to complete two years with the firm so they could become Senior Associates.

I spoke with Andrea and listened to her reasons for wanting and needing to bring these individuals in as Senior Associates, and she had some good reasons. I explained why it was posing problems for the firm – that existing employees were upset, that her offers violated firm policy, it created inequitable situations for existing employees, etc.

As we discussed possible solutions, it was apparent to me that our existing policy made it difficult for Andrea to attract top talent to the firm, and we prized top talent. I decided it was time we over-hauled our long-standing policy about requiring two years within our firm to be promoted to Senior Associate. I made a case to our Executive Committee, and the change was approved.

Debrief: Note that when I described the difficult situation. I didn't throw my co-worker under the bus – painting her as difficult to work with (which, by the way, she was!), but rather I presented her as someone passionate about her job and her drive to be successful (which, by the way, she was!). I let the hiring manager know I was flexible, open to discussion, willing to change for the right reasons. At the same time, I let the hiring manager know I felt rules and policies were important, but that the needs of the business came first, and I was willing to make changes if necessary.

Question: Tell me about a time when you wrote a report that was well received.

Answer: A few years ago, at my recommendation, our firm competed to earn a spot in *Fortune's Top 100 Companies in America to Work For.* Part of the process was to have fifty percent of our randomly selected employees complete a fairly extensive survey.

We didn't win. But as part of our feedback, we were provided a synopsis of our employees' responses to the survey, categorized in about every imaginable way possible: by length of time with the firm, men / women, age, by specific minority, job family (attorney, secretary, paralegal, etc.), etc.

I wrote a multi-page report on the results of the survey. I highlighted areas the firm scored the highest, and what I thought we were doing that caused high ratings in each of those areas. I also identified the areas we were weakest, expressed my thoughts about why we were weak in those areas, and made proposals about how to strengthen those areas.

I presented the paper first to our Executive Committee and then to the firm in a Town Hall meeting. The Executive Committee expressed appreciation for the thorough presentation and boiling down the statistics into useable data. The Town Hall meeting generated tremendous discussion and great ideas on how to improve the firm.

Debrief: This answer allowed the hiring manager to see that I was proactive (I recommended that the firm participate in the contest) and had the ability to analyze and present data in a clear and concise manner.

Additional generic questions to prepare answers for include:

Question: Tell me about a time when you:

...had to make a difficult decision with limited facts.
...when you set your sights too high (or too low).
...had a new boss or co-worker whose trust you had to gain.
...had to deal with an angry customer.
...overcame a major obstacle.
...when you had competing priorities and not enough time to do them all. How did you solve the problem?
...had to resolve a conflict between two co-workers who reported to you.
...persuaded team members to do something your way.
...creatively solved a problem.
...anticipated potential problems and prepared for them.
...used good judgment to solve a major problem.

For a list of other behavior-based interview questions, just Google that phrase (*behavior-based interview questions*) and you'll get a number of questions to think about.

Job-Specific Questions
The list of potential job-specific questions are endless, but here are a few that you might end up fielding, depending on the position for which you are interviewing.

Question: Tell me about a time when you:

... took a sales area that had been under-producing and made it produce.
... solved a difficult personnel problem.
... had to discipline a problem employee.
...debugged a difficult software problem.

…managed a construction project.

…were responsible for project managing a multi-million dollar project.

And so forth. Note that "Tell me about a time when you…" and "Help me understand how you handled…" questions are pretty popular now. They allow the interviewer to discern if you have had experience in the areas that are specific to a particular job, and how you handled yourself in certain situations.

You should also expect more philosophical-type questions:

…If we hire you, what kind of employee will you be for us?

…If I asked the people who worked for you what kind of manager you were, what would they say?

…Give me three terms that describe your management philosophy, and why.

…If you owned this company, what direction would you want the company to go in?

As important as some of these questions are, the **most important questions** for you to focus on are the questions you hope they *won't* ask — the ones you have the weakest answer for. Hoping they won't ask those questions is *not* a good interview strategy! Better to develop an answer you can live with, that will allay any (or most of the) concerns of the interviewer now, when you're not on the hot seat. While those questions are probably as numerous as there are candidates – we all seem to have at least one area of weakness – here are the types of questions you should be able to answer:

"You've been out of work for a long time. Why do you think that is?"

"You don't have nearly as much experience as some of the other candidates for this position. Why should we hire you?"

"Can you explain these gaps in your employment history?"

"Why did you leave this company after only a few months?"

These are the kinds of questions that you need to be doubly prepared to answer in an interview. Preparation up front is key to surviving this minefield. Perhaps you have good answers to those questions; if that's the case, then you should work out your answers ahead of time. Perhaps your answers are less than satisfying to you; if that's the case, you need to massage them to make sure they will pass muster.

You can't lie, of course. But how do you address the question: "Why did you leave this company after only a few months?" if the real answer is you got fired for poor performance?

Here are two possible answers to the above question:

1. I was fired for poor performance.

2. It's very hard for me to talk about this. When I took the job, it appeared to be a great fit for my skills and background. But once I got into the job, I discovered that I was in way over my head – I really didn't have the knowledge and skills necessary to do the job. That became apparent very quickly. If the company would have had time to train me or work with me, I am sure I could have come up to speed. As it was, they needed someone to be able to hit the ground running. It was a mutual decision that I leave.

What questions do I hope they won't ask?

So – which answer would you prefer giving? I know which one I would prefer hearing as a hiring manager! Even though the second answer would give me a little concern, I am by nature a pretty fair-minded person, and can see how something like that could happen.

An important concept to keep in mind is that you must sell yourself. You are the product, and the hiring manager is the customer. Look for opportunities to answer questions in the most positive, advantageous-for-the-customer way possible.

I had a friend who was unemployed for several years. On paper, he looked like a great candidate – he had a Bachelors degree in electrical engineering and an MBA. He had a decade of experience in the field in which he was seeking employment. On paper, he was as good a candidate as you could hope for. He had many interviews, but was never the selected candidate.

One day after he learned he hadn't gotten yet another job, I proposed we do a mock interview. In preparation for the interview, I asked him to write down all the questions he could remember from his most recent interview as well as any others he could remember from previous interviews.

He came by my house with a fair number of questions. I told him to answer the questions as he did in the interviews, to the best of his recollection, and I started asking him the questions. The second question I asked him was:

> "Have you ever used XYZ software?"

> "No."

> "That's it? You didn't say anything else?"

> "No."

I thought I found a clue as to why he wasn't getting any of the jobs for which he'd interviewed, so I pursued that question a little further. I asked him if he was familiar with the XYZ software, and he said yes, of course, that it was one of the more common software packages in his line of work, but that he'd never used it before. I asked if there were similar software packages that did the same thing and if he had used them. He assured me that was the case – they were critical to the achievement of the work he did. I suggested that a better answer to the software question *may* have been:

> "No, I've not used XYZ software before, but I have used ABC and DEF software packages, which do the same thing. I am very adept at software, and there's no question in my mind that I could come up to speed on XYZ software very rapidly."

As we went through his list of questions, his responses to many of them were similar to the example I provided above. Yet, even the questions he answered positively were answered briefly and sparingly – with no effort to sell himself or his abilities.

Finally, one of my favorite questions to ask candidates is:

> We have a number of excellent candidates for this position. Why should we hire you?

By the way – if you are asked that question, that is not the time to be humble. Tell the hiring manager what *you* will do for *them* if they hire you:

> Well, you should hire me because I am the best! You mentioned you needed someone to lead your HR organization, and I have been leading HR organizations for many years. I have extensive experience in benefits, compensation, recruiting and training – all areas you're concerned about. I would love to put my experience and skills to work in your organization, and I know you won't regret hiring me.

While writing this book, I interviewed a woman for a position. While she had the basic skills and qualifications we were seeking, she wasn't the best qualified candidate. When I asked her that question ("We have some strong candidates for this position — why should we hire you?") she sat up tall, looked me in the eye and said:

> No one will work as hard as I will work, and no one will be as passionate as I am about this job! I love this work and will give it my very best.

What's not to like about that answer?! (By the way – I hired her…)

My Least-Favorite Questions

There are two more questions that you will almost assuredly run into if you do much interviewing. They are questions I am not fond of, but they seem almost like a rite of passage for interviewers and candidates. Those questions are:

- Tell me about your strengths, and
- Tell me about your weaknesses.

If I could ban two questions from the interview arena (aside from illegal ones), it would be these two. I think they show a lack of imagination and may indicate poor interviewing skills. Alas, I can almost guarantee that you will run into one or the other, if not both of these questions. So it's best to be prepared for them.

The answer to the first question — about your strengths — should be evident: your strengths just happen to be exactly what the employer is looking for! You tailored your résumé to the key elements of the job and that helped you get the interview. Carry that tailoring into the interview. You can't lie, of course, but you can accentuate the positive. The job is a sales position and you've picked up during the interview or from the job description that they are especially interested in candidates who have opened new territories before? Provided you have done that before, *that* is one of the strengths you share:

> Well, Bob, I think one of the things that makes me stand out from other candidates is that I am really good at opening up new territories. In fact, in my last job I was so successful at doing that, that I was sort of the company pioneer – being sent ahead into new territories to open them.

They're looking for an exceptional finish carpenter? Then that's one of your strengths and one of the things you enjoy doing most.

Now, to my least favorite of these two least favorites: "Tell me about your weaknesses." For years, common counsel was to make a weakness appear to be a strength that will appeal to the employer:

> Well, I guess I tend to work too many hours – sometimes I get so caught up in the job that I spend more time at work than I probably should.

Or

> I guess I am a perfectionist, and sometimes I am not as patient with others who aren't.

Most interviewers will see through answers like those as a make-your-weakness-appear-as-a-strength tactic. I would prefer to answer the weakness question with a weakness that has nothing to do with the job for which I am applying. For example, when I was interviewing for the position I obtained at the City of Aurora (Division Manager of Human Resources), had I been asked this question (I was not), I would have said something like:

> Well, I think I am a little weak in international HR. There have been periods of my career that I was really good at that, but in recent years, my skills in that area have become pretty rusty.

The City of Aurora probably has no need for international HR skills, so that weakness is pretty benign and would not concern an interviewer.

My brother-in-law asked me how to handle the weakness question if he were to run into it during an interview. He had a successful career with the Marines as a Public Relations officer, and was transitioning to private industry. Most of the jobs for which he was applying were stateside and had no need of dealing with foreign governments or non-English-speaking people. The weakness we decided he would share was:

> Well, I guess my greatest weakness is that I find it difficult to keep my train of thought and a good word flow when I am speaking through an interpreter.

So, while they may not be my favorite questions, expect to run into them during your interviews, and prepare accordingly.

The Unasked Questions
Regardless of the specific questions asked, whether they are generic or job-related – bear one thing in mind – all the questions are designed to answer the following questions:

- Will this person add value to my organization?
- Can this candidate solve this very important problem I have at this time in my organization?
- Can this person help me out?
- Will this candidate fit into our culture and the team with which he or she will be working?

That pretty well distills it down.

More on Questions

There is another set of questions you should prepare: questions to ask your potential employer during the interview. Surely there are aspects of the job that you are curious about – think of around half a dozen questions to ask your interviewer. Write them down and bring them with you to the interview. Some possible questions include:

- What do you expect the successful candidate to accomplish in their first six months on the job?
- What do you think are the key attributes of the candidate who will be most successful in this job?
- How many people report to this position?
- Why is this position vacant?
- When do you think you will be making a decision?

These questions should be written down on a padfolio or pad of paper that you will be taking to your interview. More on that in the next chapter.

Note, by the way, that none of these questions has anything to do with benefits, vacation time, or salary. Your first interview is not the place to ask these questions. Asking those questions during the initial interview signals you are concerned about what's in it for you, not what you can do for their company.

If you will spend time doing and bearing in mind the things I have covered in this chapter, you will be prepared for your interview. That preparation will help you be confident as you arrive for your interview. And that is the subject of the next chapter, so read on!

Prepare good questions for the interview.

11. THE INTERVIEW

You don't win the silver medal, you lose the gold medal.
– Nike commercial

Game time!

The time for practice and drills is over – you're stepping onto the gridiron, diamond, pitch, field, mat. You've arrived – now it's time to shine.

Let me share with you some thoughts about interviewing.

First of all – congratulations for earning an interview. All your preparation has brought you to this point…now is not the time to choke.

I have a friend who is an executive recruiter. I asked him to provide me with pointers about interviewing. He said, "I teach all my candidates the 20-20-20 rule." I asked what that was, and he said:

> When you arrive for an interview, remember 20-20-20: the first 20 feet, the first 20 seconds, the first 20 words. This is where you will make your first impression – make the most of it.

I thought that was such sound advice, I decided to include it here.

The first 20 feet. What happens during the first twenty feet? To begin with, you are establishing the first impression for all who meet you. Here are a few things I can think of:

- You're on time (or not).
- You smile pleasantly.
- You are wearing your interview suit, your shoes are shined, and you look like a million bucks – you certainly look the part.

The first 20 seconds. How about:
- You greet the executive assistant or HR specialist professionally and politely.
- You sit like a professional (not sprawled on the couch, not reclining in a chair, etc.)
- You seem calm, cool, and collected.
- You shake hands firmly.
- You make eye contact and smile at all those you meet.

The first twenty words:
- Your greeting is genuine and sincere.
- You remember – and use – people's names.
- You appear calm, your speech isn't overly informal, and you seem like a pleasant person.

So – pay attention to the first twenty feet, seconds and words.

Following are a few pointers gleaned through years of interviewing candidates for positions, and from working with hiring managers and Human Resources departments.

DRESS FOR SUCCESS!
In a previous chapter I provided my thoughts on how you should dress for your interview. Be sure and put on your interview duds – you'll feel like a winner as you walk out of your house, and the proper clothing will help you feel confident as you arrive for your interview.

LOCATION
This may seem ridiculous to mention, but be sure you know where you are going for your interview. When I was in high school and college, when I asked a girl on a date, if I didn't know where she lived I always did a trial run before our date, making sure I could find her home, how long it took to get there, etc.

And so should you when you have gotten an interview. Make sure you have the address of the company. In addition to knowing what time to be there, know well *where* you are to be – what building, what floor, who to ask for, etc. The day or two before your interview, drive by the building.

When I interviewed with the law firm I worked at, their offices were located in downtown Denver, on the 41st floor. The day before the interview, I drove downtown in rush-hour traffic (since my interview was the next day at 8:30am), found where to park, and then walked into the building. I took the elevator to the 41st floor. I timed all this, and from leaving my driveway to arriving at the 41st floor, it took me 55 minutes – so basically an hour. The next day, I left my house at 6:30am – two hours before my interview. Since traffic wasn't quite as busy as the day before (since I left an hour earlier), I got there in plenty of time – I had about an hour and fifteen minutes to burn before the interview.

Fortunately, I had brought my behavior-based questions and answers with me, so I used the time to bone up on my answers and to practice them. I also had the job description, so I could refresh my memory about all the elements of my specialty they were looking for.

As the time for my interview approached, I left my car and walked to the building. I waited in the lobby the last ten minutes or so, then at about five minutes before my interview, I stepped on the elevator. I arrived at the reception desk about three minutes before my interview, and informed the receptionist I was there, and who I was to interview with.

TIMING
Now, as you read that last few paragraphs, you might be thinking, "Dan's obsessive about all this!" And yes, you would be correct. But beyond that, I cannot stress enough the importance of **being on time to your interview!** Notice I said, "on time," not "arrive early." I have to be honest, it annoys me to no end to have a candidate show up twenty or thirty minutes before the time for their interview. Often, I schedule interviews back to back. That means if you arrive twenty minutes early and my secretary calls me, you are interrupting someone else's interview. Also, even if I am not in an interview, believe me, I have plenty to do. I will not appreciate that you have arrived early. It does not signal to me your eagerness about the job – it mostly just annoys me. And it is never good to annoy the hiring manager.

As bad as arriving early, arriving late is worse. Through the years, I have had far too many candidates arrive late. Sometimes they call ahead to tell me they are stuck in traffic, or have gotten lost, or whatever. That softens the blow a bit, but it is not impressive. You see above how fixated I am about time. The fact that you are late may throw other interviews off. Or – I may interview you for half an hour instead of 45 minutes or an hour – I will short you, not the candidate after you.

If you are late for an interview, you have one strike against you before you even meet the hiring manager. If you arrive really early (ten to thirty minutes) you have about three quarters of a strike against you before you begin.

For those times when you are unavoidably late, it is good to have the company's main number as well as the number for the hiring manager with you the day of the interview. If you are running late, by all means call the hiring manager. But he or she may not be in their office – they may have other meetings, be interviewing other candidates, etc. If no one answers his or her phone, try hitting 0 and # during their voice mail message — that will often transfer you to the hiring manager's secretary, who can get a message to the manager. If 0 # doesn't work, having the main number of the company allows you to reach the receptionist, who can then get you to the manager's secretary.

But bottom line is – don't be late. You've heard the axiom *Better late than never*? Well, when it comes to interviewing, I would say: *Better never late*.

RÉSUMÉ

When you arrive for your interview, you should have brought three to five copies of your résumé with you. Carry them in a padfolio or along with a pad of paper so they don't get smudged or wrinkled. The padfolio / pad of paper also has the benefit of being something you can take

Better never late!

notes on during your interview. This isn't a must, but I always like to interview candidates who take notes during interviews. We all like to think that what we are saying is important or of interest to others.

You should bring multiple copies of your résumé for a number of reasons:

1. Bring numerous copies since there may be more than one interviewer – team interviews are very popular these days.
2. The hiring manager may have forgotten to bring your résumé to the interview.
3. Often, résumés that get cut and pasted into applications software are in plain text – no formatting, functional spacing between paragraphs, etc. The résumé you have labored over (see the earlier chapter on résumés) to present just the right image is wasted!
4. It shows you are prepared and are courteous – that you think of others.

Regardless of whether you need them, it is a good sign of your preparation and professionalism if you arrive with résumés ready for your interviewers.

BUSINESS CARDS
When you meet your interviewers, ask each of them for a business card. When they are handed to you – look at them. This will give you a moment to see the name of each interviewer (did she say Aubrey or Audrey? Kathy or Cassie?).

People's names are important to them – use them in your interview. When Kathy asks you a question, respond with, "Thanks, Kathy, that's an intriguing question…" and then answer the question.

IT'S ALL ABOUT THE COMPANY
This is something good for you to remember as you head into your interview – everything in the interview is about the company. That may seem odd – you may have been thinking it's all about you. That makes sense – they have called you, asked to interview with you, they have your résumé and application. But believe me, it is all about the company, not all about you. **Your interviewers will be evaluating your answers against what their needs are.** If your answers don't show them how you will help them solve their problems, boost their sales, increase their customer service, protect the company, etc., you will not be hired.

They will most likely *not* ask you those specific questions. But they will be listening carefully to what you say and trying to determine if you are the answer to their problems. So remember that.

Let me give you an example. Here's a pretty innocent question:

Tell me why you would like to work for our company.

If you answer something like, "I'd love to work for your company because having a job here would cut my commute in half. That's more time for me to spend with my family."

Now, there's nothing wrong with spending time with your family, but with an answer like that you missed a golden opportunity to establish yourself as the best candidate for this company. Compare that answer to this one:

I have always admired your company, and when I read the job description, I realized I have skills and abilities that will help you meet your strategic goals this year.

Or this answer:

Well, I read in the newspaper that you were expecting to bid on some new government contracts over the next few months. I have great strengths in that area, and I know that my experience in this area will be able to help you immediately.

With the first answer, you may be on your way out the door, but using the second or third answers keeps you in the game, and the interviewer will be interested in learning just how you intend to help them meet their strategic goals or how your expertise in government bidding might help them.

THE INTERVIEW
Now you're down to brass tacks. You've done all the preparation you can, from learning about the company, rehearsing answers to potential questions, dressing appropriately, arriving on time, etc. The spotlight's on, and you are on stage. Time to shine!

Often, as a warm-up question, interviewers will ask the vanilla question, "Can you tell us a little about yourself?" This is sort of an ice breaker, an opportunity to put you at ease. It is important to note that in response to this inquiry, most interviewers don't want to hear about your spouse, children, sports activities, hobbies, etc. They are really looking for how you can help them. Remember that – no matter how nice they are (and they may really be nice people), what they are really looking for is whether you can add value to the organization, solve a problem for them or help them out in some way. All your answers should be given with those things in mind.

You can use this question to answer those unasked questions, and to set the tone for the rest of your interview. I have been asked that question before, and here is my answer:

> First of all – thank you for your time today. I know you are all very busy. In answer to your question: I am an HR professional with nearly two decades of HR experience. I have a broad range of skills, from A, B and C to D, E and F (*note that where A, B, C D, E, & F are all elements from the job description, or at least those elements where I have experience*). I am passionate about HR – I love the legal and formal aspects of HR, but I also enjoy the opportunity to touch people's lives and make a difference. I've worked for Fortune 20 companies and small organizations, and feel comfortable in both settings. And that's me in a nutshell.

Look at what I just told them about me in about thirty seconds:

- I am an HR professional;
- I have nearly twenty years' experience;
- My skills range covers the areas they are looking for in the job;
- I love the technical and legal aspects of HR;
- But I also love the people aspects of HR;
- I can be succinct and get to the point.

And – did my questions answer any of the following unasked questions:

- Will this person add value to my organization?
- Can this candidate solve this very important problem I have at this time in my organization?
- Can this fellow help me out?
- Will this candidate fit into our culture and the team with which he or she will be working?

My answer addressed each of those questions in one way or another.

Listen. As you are asked questions, be sure and *listen to the entire question.* Don't be in such a hurry to answer that you cut the questioner off. I had an experience with a candidate like that – she just wouldn't let me finish a question before she jumped in with her answer. It was rather vexing. I am sure she was anxious to please and show that she really knew what she was talking about. But mostly it was off-putting.

If you don't understand a question – don't guess. Ask for clarification – there is no problem with that. Simply say, "I'm sorry, but I don't understand exactly what you are asking. Would you mind repeating the question?" Most interviewers will reword the question in a manner that will make it more understandable.

Don't be a story teller! Now I will give you some advice I need to remind myself about often during interviews. **Get to the point when you answer questions.** I have a really bad habit of telling people the history of time when they ask me what time it is, and I frequently don't get around to ever telling them the time. If you find your answers wandering around, and it's taking you a long time to get to the point of the answer, economize and get to the answer. Better yet, if you know this is a practice of yours, studiously try to get to the point quickly. Watch your interviewers – if they are getting fidgety, or cut you off mid-answer, recalculate your answer strategy. Not to do so may mean your interview will not end well for you. Save the stories and charismatic answers for when you have the job.

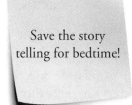

Save the story telling for bedtime!

Dangerous Questions
There are questions you must watch out for, questions that may pose problems for you. No, they aren't necessarily the questions that highlight your areas of weakness – we talked in an earlier chapter about how to prepare for and answer those questions. The questions I am speaking about are those that may inadvertently show things you don't want hiring managers to see. Questions like:

"Tell us about a time you didn't get along with a co-worker."

When answering this question, don't throw your co-worker under the bus. If you do, it may signal to the hiring manager that you are difficult to work with, or not a team player. Focus on the positive things you did to get through the situation without damaging the relationship – we discussed that in the previous chapter. If the situation that comes to mind is really a negative one that puts you in a bad light no matter how you portray it, then select another situation where you and a co-worker didn't get along. If you have worked long enough, you probably have any number of examples from which you can draw, and of course, if you have prepared for this question, you'll have just the right answer to that question.

"Tell us why you left your previous employment."

When answering this, now is *not* the time to share what an idiot or jerk your former boss was, or the poor benefits package the company offered, even if those things are true. In a recent interview, a member of the interview team I was part of asked this question, and we were stunned to hear the candidate go on and on about the terrible, illegal things her boss was doing. If that wasn't enough, she went into great detail about a disciplinary meeting she was called into and the reasons she was being disciplined. Turns out, she didn't care for the way her supervisor handled the disciplinary meeting.

Next candidate please!

"Tell us what you would do during the first six months you are here."

This is a great opportunity to share how hard you'll work, how committed to learning the organization you are, etc. It is not a time to point out the errors you think they have as an organization (even if they have expressed concern about the way they do some things). I interviewed a fellow once who basically trashed our company's compensation policy and told me how he would "clean things up" if he was to come to our company.

Your End-of-Interview Questions
At the end of the interview, hiring managers will often ask if you have any questions. Now is the time to ask the questions you have already written down (in your padfolio or on a pad of paper) and brought with you to the meeting.

There are several reasons to write your questions down. First, during the stress or adrenaline rush of the interview, you may forget what those excellent questions were that you prepared before the interview. Second, I am generally a little put off by candidates who say, "No, I can't think of any questions for you." Really? You're not the least bit curious about this or that aspect of the job?

Often, during the course of the interview, many – or even all – your well-planned questions will be answered. That's okay; but if you have written down your questions, you can scan the questions on your pad of paper (letting the hiring manager know you really did put some thought into this interview) and say something like, "Well, I had a whole list of questions to ask you, but throughout our interview, you have answered all of them." However – you'll almost always have one question:

What are the next steps?

This gives you the opportunity to find out where the company is in their hiring process, and when you might expect to hear back from them. Perhaps you are the first interview, or the last. Regardless, you should be able to learn when they will get back with you – whether for good or ill. It also provides you the opportunity to contact them if you do not hear back from them within a reasonable timeframe.

Through the years, several candidates have tried a "trial close" on me. By that, I mean they asked me something like: "Can you tell me how I stack up against your other candidates?" or "After what you've seen today during our interview, do you feel I am your top candidate?" While as a former salesman, I appreciate this, as a hiring manager I am not a big fan of it. It puts me on the spot, and I don't care for that. Having said that, I know a number of individuals whom I respect greatly, who use this tactic and have had good results with it through the years. It's just not for me.

AFTER THE INTERVIEW
Congratulations – you survived! You can breathe a sigh of relief, and now the waiting begins.

When you get home, one of the first things you should do is sit down and write a *Thank-You* note to all those with whom you interviewed. (That's another reason to get business cards during the interview.) Some experts say this is another time for you to make your case as the best candidate. However, I think it should be just what the two words on the front of the card say: Thank You. Your message should be short and to the point, something along the lines of:

> Dear Mr. Johnson,
>
> Just a quick note to thank you for your time today. I know you are busy, and I appreciate the time you spent today to help me learn more about Acme Engineering.
>
> Thank you so much for your time and consideration. If I can answer any further questions for you, please don't hesitate to contact me.
>
> Best Regards,
>
> Daniel Quillen

This should be written on a professional-looking *Thank-you* card. And remember what your mother always said – "Use your best penmanship."

When I have mentioned this tactic to people with whom I am counseling about job hunting, invariably some ask, "Won't an e-mail be easier and just as effective?"

The answer is yes and no. Yes, it's easier; no, it's not more effective. Anyone can take twenty seconds and fire off an e-mail, but a handwritten thank-you note separates you from the crowd. I'd guess about 30% of the candidates I have interviewed through the years have sent an e-mail thank you, but only 1% or 2% have sent a handwritten note. It's impressive to me. Will it make the difference? Not if you don't have the skills and qualifications required for the job. But if it's close between you and someone else, who knows? It might help.

Now get in touch with those whose names you have provided as references, and let them know they may be contacted. Tell them about the job for which you have interviewed, and if you want them to accentuate anything about you as a candidate, ask them to mention that if they are so inclined.

Follow-Up

If you don't hear something right away, when is it too soon to follow up? Part of that depends on what the next steps were going to be for the hiring manager. If s/he told you that you were one of the first to be interviewed and it would take a couple of weeks to get through the rest of the candidates, don't call a week after the interview.

If, however, the hiring manager told you that you were one of the last interviews, and they should make a decision by the end of the week, then I think you can call on Tuesday of the following week if you haven't heard anything. Tuesday isn't pushy – calling the Friday the hiring manager said they would make the decision is. When you call on Tuesday, your message should be something like:

> Hello, Mr. Johnson, Bob Jones here. I remember you mentioned you were hoping to make your decision on the Sales Manager position by last Friday, so I thought I would follow up to see if you have any further questions for me. Also, I just wanted to let you know I am still very interested in the position.

I can tell you from personal hiring experience that I am often unable to make a hiring decision in the timeframes I initially shared with candidates. Work gets busy, a candidate cancels and has to reschedule, and any number of other reasons. So be patient, and don't give up hope.

Here's something to remember – just because getting hired by that company is at the top of your importance list, chances are pretty good that it gets easily supplanted in the hiring manager's business life – filling the position is the smoke on the horizon, and while that's important, the fire at his feet is going to take precedence every time.

Having said that, it's okay to check in occasionally until you're told someone else has the job (or until you get the job), but be careful – persistence is good – it shows you are interested in the job. But there is a fine line between persistence and stalking.

Don't be a stalker!

If the manager seems evasive or quits returning your calls, assume the worst and move on. You might be pleasantly surprised, and s/he may call later than you expect to offer the job, or call you in for another interview, but don't make a nuisance of yourself.

If the call comes and – sad day – you are not the chosen candidate, be professional in your response. Don't subject the caller to a litany of questions about why your weren't chosen. It is okay to express disappointment, but be completely professional. More than once I have hired someone who didn't work out, and I went to Candidate #2. Also – more than once I hired someone who didn't work out, but I didn't call Candidate #2 because they were a complete jerk when I initially called with the bad information.

TELEPHONE INTERVIEWS

In today's fast-paced business world, many first interviews are conducted by telephone. Earlier in this book, I cited the fact that I had 31 interviews while looking for a job. Actually, I had far more than that, but I only counted one interview per company. Of those 31 interviews, over half (16) were telephone interviews (one was an interview over Skype). Sometimes it was because of distance – the recruiter or HR professional with whom I was interviewing lived in a distant city. Other times, it was a preliminary or screening interview, even though the company was located in the same city where I live.

Be sure and treat every interview with the importance it deserves – don't do any less preparation, don't be any less professional.

12. DOES AGE MATTER?

Age is an issue of mind over matter. If you don't mind, it doesn't matter.—
Mark Twain

While Mark Twain's opinion on age may be true in some areas, I am not sure I agree with him when it comes to the employment arena.

I am frequently asked if age discrimination in the workplace is real. Before my job hunt, I was of the opinion that it isn't – that HR departments and hiring managers are too smart to do that.

But now, I'm not so certain.

OLDER WORKERS

In the *Résumés* chapter, I mentioned the earliest date on my résumé was 1992. Partly that was because the positions I had before 1992 were not HR positions, and so were of limited relevance to the positions for which I was applying. However, I also did not list the older jobs so that hiring managers or screeners couldn't approximate my age – just in case that was an issue for them.

As I mentioned earlier, after my job search was completed, I had submitted 130 applications and received 31 interviews – nearly a one-in-four ratio. That ratio held pretty consistent throughout my job search. I was getting the interviews, just not the jobs.

Maybe that says something about my interviewing skills, but perhaps it was something a little more...sinister. I had been the bridesmaid on a number of jobs (others I self-selected out of because they just weren't good matches).

But when I failed to be the chosen candidate, I figured the other candidate must have been a stronger interviewer or perhaps been a better match for the position. Normally my mind does not conjure up visions of discrimination – I am just not wired that way.

But then, I had an interesting experience. A leader of one of the networking groups in which I participated reviewed my résumé and heard of the success I had been having with it. He had not been in attendance at the networking meetings I had attended, so we had not met. He called me and asked me to come present my résumé to the networking group and help them learn the secrets to my success in procuring interviews.

I attended the next meeting and presented to them. I met this gentleman. Afterwards he was pleasant and complimentary about my presentation.

A few days later, my phone rang and it was him. He identified himself and we chit-chatted for a few minutes. Then he said something like, "Dan, I am concerned that you are getting so many interviews, but not landing any of the jobs. I have seen and heard you speak, and you are very well-spoken, adept and engaging, so I don't think that's it.

"But I think I may know what your problem is. When I reviewed your résumé, I assumed you were in your early 40s, maybe 45 at the oldest. But when I met you, well, I'd guess you are closer to your mid-50s. Am I right?"

I acknowledged that was true. As I look in the mirror, I see a middle-aged, balding man. I have looked 50 for about 15 years because of my hairline. Sigh…

He continued: "Dan, I think it's a possibility you are running into age discrimination."

I realized that he was probably right. So many of my interviews had gone well – I had answered the questions brilliantly (in my estimation), felt like I had established a rapport with the interviewer, etc. But – no offers came.

He said, "Dan, I would strongly suggest you deal with this head on – that you recognize the possibility that the hiring manager holds preconceived notions about older workers that aren't very positive, and say something that will ease their mind on the subjects they can't ask you."

We discussed the topics that might be of concern to hiring managers. They included things like:

- How long is this guy going to continue working? Are we going to get him all trained and then he retires?
- I wonder how capable he is with technology? Sometimes older people have a difficult time learning new software and other technology.
- Will he be sick all the time?
- I wonder if he'll get along with younger workers? We have a lot of them at the company.

He then suggested I work up a short statement to present at the end of my interview, touching on each of those items. I did so, then e-mailed it to him for his comments. We worked together and tweaked it a bit until I was comfortable with not only the wording, but the tone. Following is what we came up with. At the point of the interview where they ask me if I have any questions, I planned to say:

> Yes, I do. But first, I'd like to share some information with you that you can't ask me. But since I am sharing it freely, there is no problem. I don't want to make you feel uncomfortable, but I would like to address a couple of topics. (By now, I had their attention!) As you may have noticed, I am not a spring chicken, and I am probably older than most of the other applicants. But I want you to know that I have a lot of runway left on my career – I am not considering retirement any time soon. I have three children who are in college for a number more years, and besides, I am nowhere near being ready to retire.
>
> **(That dispels their concern that I will retire as soon as I get trained.)**
>
> I am very good at learning new software. I have been at this so long that I have used many different software packages, and have never had difficulties picking up new applications or software packages.

(That addresses any concerns they have about whether I can learn new software or work with new technology.)

I enjoy all ages of workers and work well with younger workers as well as workers my age.

(So much for the concerns about me being a crabby old man…)

And I am very healthy. I have worked 50 hours a week for most of my career, and have no reason to expect I will work less in this position.

(And now they know I am healthy and they don't have to worry about me being sick all the time.)

In addition, the benefit to you is that you get an HR professional with years of HR experience. I have been doing HR so long, there are very few things that surprise me – I have seen it all. Because of that, I don't get too excited or agitated about anything that comes up.

(Adding a cherry on top – not only do they not have to worry about me as an older worker, but they actually benefit from it!)

For the purposes of this book, I wish I could tell you I used this approach many times. But I didn't – I used it only once. But…I am batting 1000 when using it – I got every job for which I applied when I used that dialogue.

Meet age discrimination head-on.

And now for the rest of the story….

A few months after I got my current job, I asked my boss what he thought of my little spiel about my age. I wanted to know if perhaps my statement had made him feel uncomfortable or concerned. He said that quite to the contrary, he felt it was unique and well stated. He had never heard anyone do that before, and he thought it a great idea.

Sometimes, age discrimination isn't so obvious, and is not discrimination at all. It may simply be that a hiring manager has a salary budget he or she is working with, and an older worker – with years of experience and salary progression – simply makes more than the hiring manager can afford to pay. I ran into that several times during interviews. One hiring manager told me she would love to be able to afford me, but just couldn't stretch that far. Even at the rock bottom end of my salary range, she felt she couldn't stretch that far. She ended up hiring a candidate with about one-third of my experience, and at one-third of my preferred salary.

I mentioned earlier that I tend not to blame others for my failures, but I have to admit age discrimination may have played a role in at least several jobs for which I had interviewed. Perhaps you'll run into that in your quest for work, and I hope these thoughts will help you overcome those issues.

YOUNGER WORKERS
At the other end of the age spectrum are those workers who are just graduating from college and are looking for their first career job. In a market like this, it's tough to land a position without experience. What's a bright, eager and enthusiastic young candidate to do?

Here are a few thoughts:

If you are still in school…stay there. Don't let circumstances (marriage, debt, family situations, etc.) tempt you to drop out of school before you obtain your degree. I can't emphasize that enough. Once you leave school it is very difficult to go back to resume your education. It's doable, but far more difficult than you can imagine.

If the reason for your potential educational departure is financial – there are plenty of options to cure that issue. Assuming family isn't a funding option, student loans, scholarships and grants are all available. Scores of books have been written on these topics – go to the library and check them out.

But let's assume you've graduated – what next? If you began reading at the beginning of this book, you know that this New Economy is tough to find work in, even for those with experience.

But you haven't got experience, so what do you do? My advice is to let your advantages shine through – your youthful energy, the passion you have that caused you to enter your field of study in the first place.

Most colleges have career placement offices – this is a great place to start. They'll have their fingers on the pulse of the work environment, and may even have job leads for you. They can help you massage your résumé so you can accentuate all your positives.

Many company websites have tabs for recent graduates that list jobs and internships.

A word or two about internships. Internships are wonderful opportunities to get your foot in the door of a company, and to show them how good you can really be for them. But – make no mistake — they are first and foremost a job interview – a very extended job interview. The hiring company will be evaluating you and watching to see if you are the kind of employee they want to have at their company. Your work ethic – what time you show up to work, how late you stay, your availability for projects, are all considered and evaluated.

The quality of your work is also considered. They know you haven't got experience and can't be expected to know as much as employees who have worked there for years. But they recognize half-hearted efforts and sloppy work. All your work should be packaged as though you were presenting it to the toughest grading professor at your school. No typos, sentence fragments, incomplete thoughts.

In a word (actually – in four words): *Take your internship seriously.*

Since you don't have years and years of experience, show what you do have. If a company is willing to hire new talent, you will be competing against others who have little or no experience also. Accentuate the positive!

Have you done volunteer work in the field in which you are seeking a position? List it. Chances are since you are going into a particular field, you have had experience somehow related to it. You're going into Criminal Justice and did ride-alongs with police officers? List that. You're going into veterinary medicine and worked or volunteered in a kennel or at a vet? Be sure and mention it. Hiring managers like to see you have an interest in a field long before seeking career employment in it.

A number of years ago, one of my sons was interested in working for a TV studio. He was just graduating from high school, and had a real interest in making the technology portion of theater and television his career. He had worked on the sound and lighting crews for plays for several years in high school – it was his passion. Following is the résumé he used as a high school graduate, with little paid experience in his field:

W. Michael Quillen
Address, e-mail and phone numbers
Summary

I have nearly four years of experience in creating sound design and operating sound, lighting boards and shop time. I have worked with equipment such as Machie, ETS Express, Shure, Audio-Technica, and others. In addition I have some knowledge about different soundboards and systems. I have over 800 hours of shop time recorded over 3 years. My theater experience also includes performing in outstanding plays such as *Chess, Into the Woods, Secret Garden* and *Evita*, and Stage Manager for *Little Shop of Horrors*.

I was a student intern for four months working in Lucent Technologies' business television studio. I served a variety of roles in that position, including cameraman, sound and light board designer and operator.

Qualities I possess include leadership, precision, professionalism, and the flexibility to adapt to difficult situations. I am proficient in MS Word and experienced in Excel. I am also fluent in Czech and Slovak.

Experience in Sound and Light

Show	Position	Location
Grease	Designed and Operated Board	Eaglecrest HS
Chess	Designed	Eaglecrest HS

Show	Position	Location
Anything Goes	Assisted in Operating Board	Eaglecrest HS
Count Dracula	Assisted in Design	Eaglecrest HS
Evita	Co-Designer	Eaglecrest HS
Into the Woods	Designed	Eaglecrest HS
Peter Pan	Designed and Operated Board	Eaglecrest HS
Prelude to a Kiss	Assisted in Design	Eaglecrest HS
Secret Garden	Assisted in Design	Eaglecrest HS
Steel Magnolias	Designed and Operated Board	Eaglecrest HS
The Mystery of Edwin Drood	Designed and Operated Board	Eaglecrest HS
The Wayside Motor Inn	Designed and Operated Board	Eaglecrest HS
Working	Assisted in Design	Eaglecrest HS
Lost In Yonkers	Assisted in Light Design	Eaglecrest HS
Rumors	Operated Board	So. Utah University
Business Television Studio	Sound and Light Board Intern	Lucent Technologies

Awards and Honors

Outstanding Theater Student award for 1997- 1998

Outstanding Theatre Student for Junior class (1996-1997)

The Michael Landon Award (All-around outstanding Performing Arts Student)

Outstanding Choir Student for Senior class (1997-1998)

Worked on a Foreign Exchange program with French Theatre Company (1998)

Highest Thespian Points in Cherry Creek School District (1996-1997)

One of three students selected to participate in interviewing candidates for new teacher positions at Eaglecrest HS

Voluntary representative for the Church of Jesus Christ of Latter-day Saints in the Czech Republic and Slovakia

As you can see, he didn't have a lot of experience in a paying job in the field he was seeking, but he showed all the volunteer work he had done in his high school and one semester of college. He was competing against a number of other youth applying for the same job, but his passion and interest shone through and he got the job. (I know you're curious what he ended up doing with all that sound experience…he is now a litigation attorney in Portland, Oregon!)

As you prepare your résumé, don't try to stretch to two pages, as mentioned earlier in this book. That was a *maximum* length, not a *minimum*! If you don't have two years worth of experience and education, one page is just fine.

13. AFTER YOU LAND YOUR JOB

Action is the foundational key to all success.
-- Pablo Picasso

Congratulations! You did it – you got the job! I am delighted for you.

Now – it's time to show your employer that they made the right decision. Here are a few stream-of-consciousness thoughts on this:

ARRIVE ON TIME, STAY ALL DAY

Remember the counsel my recruiter friend gives to candidates he represents? That's right, the 20-20-20 rule: the first 20 feet, the first 20 seconds, the first 20 words? I think I will revise that for those of you who have gotten your new job:

The first 20 minutes, the first 20 hours, the first 20 days.

The first 20 minutes. Your first day on the job is your opportunity to once again put your best foot forward. Be on time (actually – be early). In Chapter 8, we discussed the importance of being on time: I suggested you do a trial run to make sure you could find the employer's address so that you could be on time for your interview. It is very important for you to be on time your first day. Again – you have one opportunity to make a good first impression as the company's newest employee – do it right on your first day of work. If your interview was during the day at some time other than rush hour, I would even suggest doing another trial run during rush hour a few days before your start date to make sure you are on time. And then, on your first day of work, leave early enough that you will be there on time.

When you first interviewed with this company, you probably wore your interview suit, starched white shirt, and freshly polished shoes. If your new company's dress code is business, then that could also be your first-day-of-work clothing. However, perhaps your company is a little more relaxed than that. You may have noticed the day you interviewed that everyone was dressed in business casual attire. Don't assume that means you can come in khakis and collared shirt with no tie. What if your interview was on a Friday, and Fridays just happen to be casual in your new office? Since you'll likely begin your new job on a Monday, if you waltz in wearing business casual dress, you may really be out of place. The best way to avoid this is simply ask your boss – or his / her secretary — ahead of time what the expected office attire is.

When you first arrive, you may well be greeted by your new boss's secretary, administrative assistant, or a member of the HR staff. Be cautious with this first meeting – first impressions are being formed. You should treat everyone with respect and professionalism. If you come across as condescending or haughty with these critical administrative employees, it may take you some time to overcome that impression.

When you are shown to your new office / cubicle / desk, avoid negative verbal comparisons to your former digs: "Wow – this office is a lot smaller than my old office," or "Goodness – is this war surplus furniture?" etc. I cannot tell you how many times I have heard from a new employee what a nicer office they had at their old company, the lighting was better, the office was larger or had a better view, etc. I am here to tell you that is *not* very impressive. Even if you feel that way, don't set yourself up to be labeled as a complainer / whiner. If you must mention it to someone, then tell your spouse, significant other, or your parents, but keep it out of the work place.

Be pleasant and flexible. If things aren't quite ready when you arrive – office isn't clean and available, phone and/or computer isn't ready, etc., be gracious and understanding. Don't make a scene, don't demand action, etc. Just chill out. This may seem like a silly thing to caution about, but believe me, I have seen temper tantrums thrown by new employees over just these sorts of things.

In a nutshell, remember you'll be making a lot of new first impressions in your first twenty minutes on the job. Take it seriously and do it well.

The first 20 hours. The first twenty hours at your new job represent the better part of your first three days there. There is a lot to do during these three days to establish yourself.

First of all, meet everyone you can during these first few days. Hopefully someone will be there to show you around and introduce you. If your boss or a new co-worker doesn't offer, ask them to introduce you to key people: co-workers, individuals in departments with whom you will be working, etc.

Lacking that support – if your manager is out of town, doesn't have the time, etc. — don't be dismayed. Take it upon yourself to meet others in your work area. A firm handshake and a warm smile go a long way to establishing yourself within work groups.

People's names are important — learn them. Use them. Do whatever it takes to learn names quickly.

Pay attention to important paperwork – some companies require you to make your benefits selections within the first few days you are there. The omnipresent I-9 is a government form every US employer is required to have for each new employee within three days of their start date. I cannot tell you how annoying it is to have to practically stalk new employees to get them to bring in the required document proving they are eligible to work in the United States. Through the years, I have actually had to tell some new employees they couldn't return to work until they did so with the required documentation for their I-9. Seriously? That's not the way to make a good first impression. The HR department will not be happy (and you want to keep HR happy, by the way!), your boss will be miffed that you don't come to work on your third day, etc.

Speaking of I-9s, when you begin your new job, you will have to bring documentation proving you have the right to work in the United States, and your employer is required to have your I-9 completed within your first three days of work. I suggest that you show up on Day 1 with the required documentation. Your HR department will tell you that you have to provide certain documentation. The law prohibits them from telling you exactly what you need…they must simply point you to the options you have. There are a number of possible documents and / or combinations of documents that will work. The best document to have is a current passport – it contains all the information necessary. If you don't have a current passport, you can provide other forms of documentation, including:

List A
- US passport or passport card
- Permanent Resident card or Alien registration receipt card
- Foreign passport with an I-551 stamp or temporary I-551 notation

List B
- Driver's license
- ID card issued by a federal or state entity
- School ID card
- Voter's registration card
- US military or draft card

List C
- Social Security card (unless it specifically says it does not authorize employment in the United States)
- Birth certificate issued by a governmental authority
- Native American tribal document

The List A documents are stand-alone documents – any one of them meets the necessary requirement. If you don't have something from List A, then you need one item from List B *and* one from List C. (**Note:** The lists above are not exhaustive. You can get more information by Googling *I-9 required documentation.*)

By the way — do *not* think that your employer might not require this, so you'll just wait and see. Every employer who does business in the United States is required to do this. Show your employer and their HR organization what a savvy and knowledgeable employee you are, by showing up with the required paperwork.

> Bring my documents required for I-9 on Day 1

When I worked at the law firm, my team used to do benefits orientations the first morning of a new hire's start date. On occasion, my assistant would come back to her office shaking her head. "I give him six months," she would say. Then she would relate how difficult and demanding the person was, how unwilling to listen to or take instruction, how much of an entitlement mentality the person had (particularly bad in law firms with attorneys, but not limited to the legal industry). My assistant was uncanny in predicting who would last at the firm and who would not, or who would last but would be a pain to work with their entire career. I always wished I could have devised a means of holding the benefits orientation prior to the firm making an offer – we might have saved the firm big money and a lot of headaches!

So my counsel is – don't be a headache. Your goal the first 20 hours is to continue that good impression you made during your interview and your first 20 minutes.

The first twenty days. Your first twenty days on the job encompasses your first month there – hopefully the first of many to follow. I know I sound like a broken record, but this is your opportunity to continue making that first impression you started in the first twenty minutes and the first twenty hours. You'll get your first assignment, first project, conduct your first meeting, etc. Approach these with vigor and professionalism, and make sure you nail each task.

During your first twenty days (and beyond that, actually) you will have a unique opportunity – as the "new kid on the block" you can ask things like, "Why do you do that?" without sounding like a complainer or trouble maker. Often, your questions will help people relook at processes and procedures, and may be the beginning of streamlining operations. A story comes to mind....

> Once, a young couple was married. On their first holiday together, they were busily making dinner. The young husband laid the dinner ham on the cutting board and cut the ends off the ham. His wife said, "Why do you cut the ends off the ham?" He answered, "I don't know. My mom just always did that. I'll call her and ask her why she did that."
>
> The husband calls his mom and posed the question. She says, "You know, I don't know why. Grandma always used to do that, so I just started doing it too. I'll ask her."

She called her mother and posed the question. Her mother responded, "I cut the ends of the ham off because the pan was too small."

Sometimes, processes and procedures get started to answer a specific question or overcome a concern. As time goes by, sometimes those questions or concerns are no longer valid, but because no one thought about it, the process has continued in that manner, even though the need has long since been gone.

As the new kid on the block, you have a golden opportunity here, to see if you can change your culture and streamline processes.

A word of caution here, however: you need to respect history. Even with your questioning, it is important to respect what has been done in the past. Even though it isn't obvious to you as the newcomer, there may be very good reasons why things are done the way they are done.

I enforced a three-month rule on myself when I started my new job. As I encountered processes or procedures I didn't understand, I would ask my questions. But before suggesting or implementing new policies, I gave myself time to understand the larger picture – get a sense for the surrounding context of the issues. I started a document called *Opportunities*; whenever I ran across a process or procedure I didn't understand, or that concerned me, I entered them in this document. It was a memory aid so that I didn't lose the thought.

It is interesting to note that some of the things I entered in my *Opportunities* document early during my employment, when I revisited them later, didn't seem like such big issues, now that I understood the context surrounding the reasons for the decisions that had been made by my predecessors, or by individuals from other departments.

During your first twenty days, you should strive to earn the reputation as a hard and competent worker. Don't sacrifice quality for quantity, but strive to finish projects ahead of deadlines and with zero quality issues. Arrive early and leave late. You don't necessarily have to stay until 7:00pm every night, but also, don't endanger anyone who steps in front of your office door at 5:00pm. If you take a bus or ride the train to work, and have to leave at

5:05pm or 5:30pm to catch the next train, opt for the later train. It is easier to relax a work schedule than to change an early impression that you are a clock watcher. That is never a good reputation to have.

If you are an hourly employee, you have to be cautious with that last bit of advice – you don't want to be viewed as someone who pads their hours. Sometimes it's a balancing act.

Your first twenty days is the time to begin reforming your networks. One of the things I feel most vulnerable about when transitioning to a new job is the loss of my information networks, whether individuals or documents. I will never know everything there is to know about a certain job; but part of my strength is identifying and using information networks. If you're the same way, start quickly identifying and cultivating those networks.

> Make a good first impression! Remember: 20-20-20

Bottom line – your first twenty minutes, hours, and days should be filled with doing impressive things. Work hard. Keep your nose to the grindstone, head in the game, shoulder to the wheel and all the other bodily metaphors you can think of that mean: *work hard*.

WHAT IF…?

Through the years, I have counseled many job hunters who suddenly found themselves with an embarrassment of riches – two or more job offers. I've also spoken with those who had accepted an offer, only to have another, better offer come along between the time of their first offer acceptance and starting their job. I've even worked with individuals who received another offer after they had started another job.

What do you do? I will answer that conundrum in six words:

Do what is best for you.

Until about ten years ago, I would have considered some of the advice I will now provide as heresy and frankly, disloyalty. However, when it comes to Corporate America, unfortunately, loyalty is a one-way street. For many years, I was a "Company Man" – fiercely proud of my company and incredibly loyal. Little by little, my loyalty was tested. It probably began with my Executive Vice President, who counseled "Plan to stay, prepare to leave." Then, after wave after wave of layoffs hit my corporation, I saw the devastation those layoffs caused in the lives of people who were hard working, honest, and loyal employees. (And of course, as an HR professional, I was often the face and voice of the difficult news that someone was being laid off, so perhaps that colors my perspective somewhat!) I came to believe that corporations will use you and appreciate your loyalty until it is financially in their best interest to cut you loose, and then they will turn your life upside down without hesitation. If you think it can't happen to you – think again.

In 2009, my eldest son graduated from law school. That year turned out to be the worst on record for law school graduates. Law schools that were accustomed to having 95% or more of their graduating classes be fully employed within six months of graduation found their placement numbers dipping into the 40% and 30% levels. It was a tough time for graduating law students.

Despite the difficult environment, my son was fortunate enough to secure a job offer. Through networking, he learned of a position, interviewed, and was offered a job prior to the traditional on-campus interviews (OCIs) that were conducted by regional law firms at his law school. I counseled him to be sure and participate in the OCI process, even though he already had a job offer. He resisted, feeling it would be disloyal. I encouraged; he resisted. OCIs came and went, and he did not participate. Then, two weeks after the OCIs were history, the firm that offered him a job rescinded their offer, leaving him with...nothing. (See – you should always listen to your ol' Dad...!). So much for loyalty.

Therefore, my counsel is to do what is best for you and your family. Do not let some idealistic sentiment cause you to turn down an opportunity that is better for you.

But how do you gracefully do that? Well, it's not easy, and you must do all you can not to burn bridges in the process. To rescind an acceptance (if companies can rescind offers, it is only fair that you can rescind an acceptance), you might say something like:

"At the same time I was interviewing with your company, I was interviewing with XYZ Corporation. Yesterday, they called with an offer for me to come work for them. It was a very difficult decision, but after weighing it carefully, I feel it is an opportunity I simply cannot turn down. I feel bad, as I was looking forward to working with you and your company."

When rescinding your acceptance, be sure not to call your boss's baby "ugly." The reason for your decision had to do with the exceptional opportunity, the better fit you felt, etc., from the other company – not because the other company was better, but because *for you* it was better.

Some employers will be miffed – you can't help that. I rather think most will understand, although they'll be disappointed.

It is of course more difficult after you have started a new job, but to me, the same principle applies – do what is best for you and your family.

14. TEMP AGENCIES – YES OR NO?

I have come to accept the feeling of not knowing where I am going. And I have trained myself to love it. Because it is only when we are suspended in mid-air with no landing in sight, that we force our wings to unravel and alas begin our flight. And as we fly, we still may not know where we are going to. But the miracle is in the unfolding of the wings. You may not know where you're going, but you know that so long as you spread your wings, the winds will carry you.
– C. JoyBell C.

I am often asked whether job seekers should look into or use temporary agencies. That's an easier question asked than answered, but here's my take.

I have two arguments against agencies. The first is that if you do find a temporary job, you will not be able to spend forty hours each week looking for other full-time work. The second is that if you go from temporary job to temporary job, it may dilute your résumé. When I considered candidates that had a history of temporary or contract jobs, I didn't count that time as I would had they been at that same employer in a full-time employee capacity.

I have found that sometimes people will register with a couple of agencies, and then sit back and wait for them to do the work of finding a job for them. That's bad – you can use them as a tool in your job search, but they should not be the only tool you are using.

Those concerns notwithstanding, I also have to say I think temporary agencies are often overlooked by job hunters, and they are a viable way to:

GET A JOB!

1. Bring a few bucks in while you seek full-time employment,
2. Get your foot in the door of a company.
3. Keep your skills honed for that perfect job.

Let me discuss each of those items:

Bring a few bucks in the door. Depending on how sound you are financially at the time of your lay-off, or the sweetness of the severance package you are given, you may truly need to take anything that will help bring a few dollars in the door. If you are like many Americans, you are stretched pretty thin financially. Having the funds coming in from a temporary job may make all the difference – the ability to keep your home and car, for example.

Generally speaking, you won't make nearly as much working for a temp agency as you would if you were working at the company as a full-time employee – the company has to pay your salary, as well as extra to add to the bottom line for the temp agency.

Get your foot in the door. As an employer, I like using temporary agencies to hire talent. It allows me a "test drive" of an employee before determining if they have the skills, work ethic, and attitude I want and expect of my employees. Through the years, we have had many temporary employees come through the door who we eventually hired as a full-time employee. Conversely, there were also a number we thought, "Good heavens – I am so glad we didn't hire her!"

Keep your skills honed. Face it, the longer you are out of work, the more likely it is that your skills will begin to suffer. And whether that is the case, from the perspective of employers, they will be concerned that a long time off the job may impact the contribution you can make to their company, and they will question whether you can "hit the ground running." A temporary job, although not as good as a full-time job, still shows the employer you were out there in the market, performing the kind of work that they need at their company.

Consider temp agencies.

So – bottom line, I think signing up with temporary agencies is a great option, as long as you don't use them as your *only* option. If you are working forty hours a week at a company through a temp agency, that makes it more difficult to conduct your job search, but if you are focused on putting in at least a few extra hours each evening and pretty full days on the weekend, then I think they are fine.

My recommendation regarding temporary agencies is that you sign up for several different agencies — don't just choose one. Sign up with as many as three to five agencies. Each one has a different set of clients, and the job requests they receive from the business community vary from agency to agency. Therefore, it would be wise for you to sign up with several of them.

15. THE NEW ECONOMY & YOU

Success doesn't come to you, you go to it. – Marva Collins

If you are out of work – whether recently or for some time – you simply *must* understand the realities of the New Economy, and plan your strategy accordingly. Not doing so will ensure that you will spend an extended period of time looking for work.

And what are the realities of the New Economy? The New Economy is this: an economy plagued by continuing stubborn unemployment that is roughly twice what the government tells us it is. It is serious *under*-employment, an economy that is fragile and makes investors and business owners extremely cautious, and it makes for a tough environment for job seekers. It's hundreds of applicants for jobs, over-worked HR departments, and a tough path to hiring managers.

If you do not approach your search for employment in the New Economy differently that you have done prior to 2009, the chances for your success are slim. But if you utilize the strategies, techniques, and tactics I recommend throughout the pages of this book, you will increase your chances of ending your unemployment many times over.

And I know what I am talking about: I have led HR departments for more than twenty years, and have been a hiring manager for longer than that. Perhaps most important, I faced the New Economy head-on, walking in the shoes of the unemployed – your shoes — during the worst of the Recession – and I got a job. These experiences make me uniquely qualified to write this book and provide you with recommendations that will end your season of unemployment sooner than later.

As one who has walked in your shoes, I know the feelings, the emotions, the fears that go along with unemployment. I know the frustration of never hearing back from an employer whose job posting fits exactly what I can do and do well. I have felt the sting of a decision coming down to me and another candidate, and losing out. I have been there, and the advice I share throughout *Get a Job!* will help you turn those feelings of fear, anger, and depression to exultation as you secure employment.

I beat this New Economy – and I can help you do the same. The techniques and tactics I shared through the pages of this book will help you end your unemployment.

The question on most everyone's mind when they are laid off is, "What do I do now?" Many of the unemployed have families and mortgages, car payments, and other financial obligations that need to be addressed. Few of us today are care- or obligation-free. I shared insights about how to shepherd your resources during this belt-tightening time. If you are fortunate enough to leave with a severance package, you may have a little cushion; however, you should consider that your cushion will be gone sooner than you realize, so it's important for you to become very judicious in your spending.

For those who have reached the end of their cushion, or who were laid off with no more than their final paycheck, things can be dicier. I provided information about what to expect from unemployment benefits – and what not to expect. For a spell, these benefits can be your cushion. But you should work as hard as you can to find employment so you do not have to depend on that for long. Even at its best, unemployment benefits provide only a portion of the pay which you lost.

As you face life without a job, in addition to marshalling your financial resources, you must align your job-hunting resources. Networks are critical to your success in seeking and securing employment. Members of your network can provide job leads, carry your résumé to a hiring manger, and provide character references for you. As an HR professional I *always* try to find someone I know and trust who knows something about the candidates I interview. It is scary to make a major hiring decision based on a two-page résumé and a 45-minute interview. If I can find someone who can attest to a candidate's moral character, work ethic, and interpersonal skills, I feel much more comfortable about that candidate. And that is before as well as after the interview. I have interviewed and hired candidates who were not quite as qualified as others, simply because I received an endorsement from someone I trusted. And as detailed earlier in this book, I had a ten-year career in the legal industry because a member of my network provided positive support for my candidacy.

A crucial network that might not seem immediately apparent to you is your social network – the friends, family, colleagues, and work associates you'll find among your Friends on Facebook, Connections on LinkedIn and Tweeple on Twitter. I advised that you use those social networks – and showed you how — to get the word out that you are seeking employment, and to ask for assistance in your job search. Ignoring these social media avenues could result in missed opportunities – and employment – for you.

Before the New Economy rolled in and set up shop, most job hunters had reasonable success with one squeaky-clean résumé that could be used for every application, but this is no longer the case. HR departments, recruiting applications software, and hiring managers are inundated with résumés – you must make yours stand out. Not doing so ensures you will be unsuccessful in leaping to the top of the interview pile. You have mere seconds to get the attention of hiring managers, HR departments, and recruiters (nano-seconds in the case of applications software). Following the tips I provided in the *Résumés* chapter will multiply your chances for success at least three to five times.

You learned that tailoring your résumé to a particular job is critical, but you also have to take it several steps further in this New Economy – you must use the company's language (found in the job description), and fill your résumé with accomplishments – examples that not only show you have done the job they are looking to fill, but you have excelled at it.

While you may not have considered it in the past, the *look* and *feel* of your résumé are important too – don't overlook this important aspect of crafting an effective résumé. I shared my own résumé (and offered to let you use my format for yours) and discussed each of the sections in the résumé – those sections that should be there, sections that shouldn't, and those that might be. I also shared my recommendation as an HR professional and hiring manager who has reviewed tens of thousands of résumés about what sections should *not* be included in your résumé – and why.

Some may think that if you have a well-crafted, tailored résumé, that means you do not need a cover letter. If you were in that category prior to reading *Get a Job!*, I hope I have convinced you that ignoring the cover letter may get you passed over as a candidate. Don't take that chance in this New Economy! As pointed out earlier in the book, many hiring managers and HR departments only read cover letters, and only go to the candidate's résumé if their interest is piqued by the cover letter. Don't be left out in the cold because you didn't take a few extra minutes to put together a door-opening cover letter. The best résumé in the world doesn't help if it isn't read.

I drew from my personal experience with job loss during the New Economy in the *Stay Positive!* chapter. Yes, I am a cock-eyed optimist, and so it's probably easier for me than for others to maintain a positive attitude. But at this difficult time in your career, a positive approach to your life in general and your job hunt in particular may be the difference between success and failure. I have received e-mails and cover letters from candidates who I could tell were depressed or even desperate. I am sorry to say, those are not emotions or qualities hiring managers look for.

That sounds harsh, but it's true. If you can remain positive, that will carry over into your communications with hiring managers – whether through e-mail or cover letters. Negative feelings may even cause you to say, "Oh, what's the use? Why should I apply for this job? It will only result in another rejection." You will lose out on every single job you do not apply for – the answer will always be "No."

But by following the strategies I share in *Get a Job!*, you can feel confident that your efforts will help set you apart from the crowd of job seekers looking to knock you out of the competition. Let that confidence add to your positive attitude, and it will serve you well.

This New Economy has spawned a new obstacle for job seekers to overcome – Gatekeepers. Gatekeepers are anyone whose job is to keep you away from the hiring manager, the interview, and ultimately, your new job. Oh sure, they do let a few candidates through their defenses – but it's typically a very small percentage of those who apply for a position. These gatekeepers include applications software programs designed to cull out as many candidates as possible, making the job of screening résumés easier for the next gatekeepers – HR departments. Executive assistants can be yet another layer of gatekeeper that is very effective in directing traffic away from hiring managers. I address all of these gatekeepers in the book, and provide recommendations for how to hurdle them and get to your destination – the hiring manager, and hopefully, the job for which he or she is hiring.

Interviewing in this New Economy is also different than in the past, even the very recent past! Before you even get to the interview which your newly minted and tailored résumé got you, you have work to do. You *must* find out all you can about the company with which you are interviewing. What are their strategies, what markets are they entering or abandoning, and how can you assist that company in either scenario? Alert your networks that you have an interview and with whom — see if anyone in your network knows someone at the company who would be willing to give your candidacy two thumbs up to the hiring manager. Know how to get to the interview location, and plan your trip to get you there on time and ready for your interview.

I recommended an exercise for you to maximize your preparation for the interview – pondering about the questions you think will be asked, writing them down, and then answering each question – in writing. I advised that you think of the questions you will have the hardest time answering, the questions you hope they don't ask you — whether it is why you left your previous job, why the company should select you when so many others have more experience or education than you, or any other question that may expose a weakness in your candidacy. As good as you are at answering the other questions that might come your way, you *must* prepare to answer those questions that will be the most difficult for you.

If you prepare as I have counseled, you will arrive at your interview confident and self-assured. I shared critical elements of having a successful interview – arriving on time at the right office, being pleasant and profes-sional with all whom you meet – including the receptionist and executive assistant. Presenting and maintaining a professional persona while you wait, as well as when you are being interviewed, is an element you must pay attention to. These things have always been important, but are especially critical these days when the number of applicants per job has grown exponentially.

Perhaps the most important guidance I provided about interviewing successfully is that you must be keenly aware that the interview is not about *you* – it is about the *company*. HR departments and hiring managers want to know what *you* can do for *them*, not what *they* can do for *you*. Will you be able to solve this huge problem they have? If you join their team, will you be able to help them reach their strategic goals?

In many industries, the New Economy has made temporary agencies a valuable and effective tool for job seekers to consider. With the horrific economy, employers must weed through many applicants for each position. Many turn to temporary agencies to get help, and the time those individuals work for them is nothing more than a weeks- or months-long job interview. I know – as an HR professional, I have done that many times. It's kind of nice to test-drive candidates for awhile and see how they react in various situations, how they relate to team members, the quality of their work, their work ethic, and so on.

And that's *Get a Job!* Drawing on my lengthy experience as an HR professional and as one who was laid off in the midst of the worst US economy in over seven decades, I provide thoughts, guidance, recommendations, warnings and hope through the pages of this book. I like to help people, and I have a special affinity for those who need help finding work.

Best of luck in your job hunt. I am confident that my advice in these pages will help you beat the odds and rapidly enable you to rejoin the ranks of the employed. Let me know how your hunt is going, and when you find a job, I want to celebrate with you! You may reach me at wdanielquillen@gmail.com.

INDEX